Making Computers Talk: An Introduction to Speech Synthesis

Ian H. Witten

Man-Machine Systems Laboratory
Department of Computer Science
University of Calgary

Prentice-Hall, Englewood Cliffs, New Jersey 07632

Editorial/production supervision
  and interior design: *Sophie Papanikolaou*
Cover design: *Ben Santora*
Manufacturing buyer: *Gordon Osbourne*

© 1986 by Prentice-Hall
A Division of Simon & Schuster, Inc.
Englewood Cliffs, New Jersey 07632

Printed in the United States of America
10 9 8 7 6 5 4 3 2 1

ISBN   0-13-545690-8   025

Prentice-Hall International (UK) Limited, *London*
Prentice-Hall of Australia Pty. Limited, *Sydney*
Prentice-Hall Canada Inc., *Toronto*
Prentice-Hall Hispanoamericana, S.A., *Mexico*
Prentice-Hall of India Private Limited, *New Delhi*
Prentice-Hall of Japan, Inc., *Tokyo*
Prentice-Hall of Southeast Asia Pte. Ltd., *Singapore*
Editora Prentice-Hall do Brasil, Ltda., *Rio de Janeiro*
Whitehall Books Limited, *Wellington, New Zealand*

Contents

Appendix   Commercial Speech Output Devices   **140**

Subject index   **148**

Preface

Voice is an attractive alternative or complement to visual output of information from computers. It is also inexpensive: an abundance of low-cost devices for voice output—and consumer electronic products that use them—are marketed. For a few dollars you can now buy what until recently was only available as equipment for specialists in speech research laboratories. With the technology in place, more and more people need to know about computer speech: the different ways of producing it and their advantages and disadvantages, how it is used in actual products, what special interactive techniques suit speech-output systems, what components the market offers. Some of these people will be designing and implementing speech systems, others evaluating alternatives with a view to purchasing a product that uses speech, still others simply interested in keeping up with this exciting, burgeoning technology.

This book aims to spread understanding of the technical and human problems involved when speech is used as a computer output medium. It covers all levels of speech synthesis from generating the speech waveform right up to problems of intonation, pronunciation, and text understanding. In order to achieve this goal, it supplies examples of systems that use voice output, describes representative commercial products for speech synthesis, introduces relevant aspects of phonetics and linguistics, and enunciates programming principles for man-computer interaction using speech.

Along with this broadly-based approach, a number of specific techniques are described, including procedures for joining segments together at the word, syllable, and phonetic level; algorithms for automatic synthesis of intonation and rhythm; and approaches to computer pronunciation of English. This information has hitherto been inaccessible to the non-specialist without interdisciplinary training in linguistics, computer science, and electronics. An appendix reviews speech output devices presently on the market, to put the techniques and trade-offs involved into a practical, commercial perspective.

The level of the book is suited to the technically-minded layperson with a general scientific or engineering background. Although considerable use is made of terms and concepts in linguistics and phonetics, all are explained within the text. An interest in computers is essential; previous exposure to computers (at the level of "computer literacy") is helpful. Specific software, hardware, or mathematical skills are definitely *not* required.

To achieve balanced coverage of the full spectrum of computer speech, the topic is divided into four conceptual levels and a chapter is devoted to each. The initial chapter introduces the components of a speech system in terms of these levels, and outlines the human speech production process and how linguists specify the sounds of speech. The lowest level, the signal level, concerns ways of generating the speech waveform, by direct recording/playback, by parametric description in terms that can be related to the human vocal tract, or by sound-segment synthesis based on linguists' classifications of speech sounds. At the next, or segment level, individual pieces—which may be words, syllables, or phonemes—are joined together. The third, or utterance level, tackles the many problems involved in getting artificial speech to sound more natural by working on the pitch and rhythm of utterances. Pronunciation of speech from text is also a concern here, as is the difficult business of interpreting text automatically in an attempt to emulate the human art of elocution. The final level of interaction and systems involves programming principles for natural interaction with computer systems using speech output, and examples of actual systems that employ this technology. An appendix reviews the great variety of speech synthesis components that are already on the market to give an idea of the range available and how to organize it when faced with the task of selecting a suitable device.

Acknowledgments

I would like to thank the many friends and colleagues—too numerous to name individually—who have worked with me on aspects of computer speech. I owe a special debt of gratitude to David Hill and Brian Gaines, who have nurtured my interest and understanding in speech synthesis, and patiently and generously assisted my development in numerous other ways over the years. John Cleary and Phil McCrea carefully read the manuscript and made a number of useful suggestions and constructive criticisms. I have been fortunate in obtaining support for my speech research in Britain from the Science Research Council and the Government Communications Headquarters, and in Canada from the Natural Sciences and Engineering Research Council and Bell-Northern Research, as well as from the Department of Electrical Engineering Science, University of Essex, and the Department of Computer Science, University of Calgary. Finally, and above all, thank you, Pam, for everything.

1

Why Make Computers Talk?

Why make computers talk? That's a good question. Although every day we speak and listen a lot, we probably don't absorb as much information through our ears as we do through our eyes. In fact, we trust vision more. When you want to find something out for certain, it's nice to see it in "black-and-white" rather than its being "just hearsay." Most learning is done by reading or looking at pictures and diagrams. After all, you're *reading* these words. Would you have preferred this book on tape? Probably not. We can't expect that making computers talk will solve all the problems of communicating with them. What it can do is enrich the possibilities for communication by providing an alternative, or a complement, to printed output and the computer screen.

Let's consider how to take advantage of the speech medium. One good reason for listening to a radio news broadcast instead of spending the time with a newspaper or television is that you can listen while bathing, washing up, or looking after the kids. Speech leaves hands and eyes free for other tasks. Unlike television, it radiates in all directions, so a free line of sight is not needed. Because of this it is extremely useful as a secondary medium, for status reports and warning messages, in systems whose primary output is visual. Occasional interruptions by voice do not interfere with other activities, unless they demand unusual concentration. It is easy and natural for people to listen to spoken messages, remember them, and recall them later when they have time to deal with them.

Another virtue of speech communication is its portability. Telephones are everywhere. Of course, with special equipment, you don't need speech to take advantage of telephones for information transfer. A personal computer and a coupling box can provide visual communication with computer databases over the telephone. But speech needs no tools other than the telephone itself, and this gives it a big advantage. You can go into a phone booth anywhere in the world, carrying no equipment at all, and have access to your computer within seconds. Even in the wilderness you need only a portable radio transceiver. The problem of getting information into the computer is still there: Perhaps your computer system has a limited word recognizer, or you use the touchtone telephone keypad. You can do this on a dial phone with a calculator-sized tone generator. Easy remote access without special equipment is a unique dividend of speech communication.

The next benefit of speech output is that it is potentially very cheap. Being all-electronic, except for the loudspeaker, speech systems are well suited to high-volume, low-cost manufacture as integrated circuits or *chips*. Other computer output devices need either mechanical moving parts, if they are printers, or a television screen. They are therefore relatively expensive. Compare the price of a cheap TV, or an electric typewriter, with that of a cheap radio. This cost advantage was realized quickly by the computer hobbies market, where speech output peripherals have been selling like hotcakes since the mid-1970s.

A further point in favor of speech is that it is natural-seeming and somehow cuddly when compared with printers or television-style terminals. This would have been much more difficult to swallow before talking toys like Texas Instruments' "Speak 'n Spell" came along in the late 1970s. Now it is an accepted fact that friendly computer-based gadgets can speak. There are talking pocket watches that really do "tell" the time, talking microwave ovens, talking pinball machines, and talking calculators. Maybe the appeal stems simply from the novelty of artificial speech—it is still a gimmick. Also, it is obviously connected with cost. Cheap gadgets are bound to seem more friendly than expensive ones!

1.1. THE COMPONENTS OF A SPEECH SYSTEM

Let's take a look at the components of a speech output system. We will examine the problems of making computers talk at four different levels. Each level corresponds to a different chapter in this book, which describes and analyzes devices and procedures that operate at that level. As you go up the hierarchy, you have to take increasingly more sophisticated considerations into account, and it becomes more and more difficult to do this in a practical system. But that doesn't stop us from looking at the sort of things that need to be done at these higher levels.

1.1.1. The Signal Level   At the bottom is the actual process of generating a speech waveform. There are lots of devices to do this—starting with the

ordinary domestic tape recorder. To make computers talk, we must place the tape recorder under computer control. Although this can be done with analog tape recorders, there are lots of advantages to using a digital version of the speech waveform instead of analog recordings on ordinary acoustic tape.

One of the problems with straightforward digitized speech is that it is not very flexible. It's difficult to cut and splice waveforms to make new utterances out of old ones. Another drawback is that quite a lot of data is needed, even for short stretches of speech. Although this may not matter if you are using a large or medium-sized computer, many applications of talking computers are in hand-held devices like toys or calculators. Then it becomes quite difficult to store enough speech if it is recorded as a simple digitized waveform.

For this reason it may be worth storing a compressed form of the speech wave. Using digital technology makes it easy to implement sophisticated algorithms for compression. If done in the right way, this can also make the stored speech more flexible. For example, you might want to join together individually recorded words or syllables. You will sometimes need to merge one word into another to prevent a perceptible discontinuity at the junction. You will want to apply a homogeneous intonation to the complete utterance, so that the speech sounds more intelligent than just a list of words. This kind of manipulation is not possible if the raw digitized waveform is stored, but it is with some higher-level representations.

Chapter 2 discusses the drawbacks to direct recording methods in more detail. It also looks at three different commercial devices that you can buy to generate artificial speech from higher-level, more compressed, and more flexible representations. We are concerned not so much with the internal workings of these devices, but with what sort of representations they use and how you control them.

1.1.2. The Segment Level

Now that you know how to produce a speech waveform, how do you make the computer say what you want it to? Of course, you could still use a tape recorder. But the problem then is that everything it says must be prerecorded. If you are looking for something more flexible than this, the best way to proceed seems to be to make big utterances by joining smaller ones together. You make written sentences by putting words together. And you make words by putting letters together. With speech, you make utterances by joining sounds together. The key question becomes, what are the basic units?

This is what we look at in Chapter 3. Words seem to be the obvious candidate, and many systems do use them. But you have to think carefully about what you mean by a *word*. Many, if not most, of the words we use in English come from a basic stem, with different endings for singular and plural, present and past tense, noun and adjective, and so on. Should these variations all be considered different words? If so, there are very many of them, and it would be a big job to record enough to allow the computer to say a reasonable variety of things. On the other hand, if we record stems and endings separately, then we have to face the problems of joining them together. Perhaps we might as well use syllables as the basic units in the first place.

Joining syllables together is not easy. Acoustically, a lot of action happens where one syllable meets another. It is hard to get a smooth transition. In fact, it would be easier to join the pieces together in the middle of syllables, where the vowel is, because it's much easier to make smooth transitions between vowel sounds than between consonants.

These arguments are bringing us towards smaller and smaller basic units, from words to syllables, and from syllables to half-syllables. Why not bite the bullet and consider joining individual *letters* together? This would need a much smaller vocabulary of pieces—twenty-six letters instead of thousands of syllables or tens of thousands of words. Well, we are talking about speech, not writing, so we should be thinking of sounds rather than letters. Some letters are pronounced differently in different contexts. We need to use *phonemes* rather than letters as the basic units of speech. We will discuss phonemes later in this chapter. They are essentially letter-sized units, but there are rather more of them— about forty.

Things are not quite as simple as taking a recording of each of the forty-odd phonemes and joining them together in the appropriate order to make the computer talk. There are quite complicated contextual effects of one phoneme on another. In fact, it is better to generate the phonemes synthetically, rather than as a recording. There is plenty of published data which measures the important features of different phonemes, and this can be used as a base for synthetic speech. Two actual programs for making speech in this way are discussed in Chapter 3.

1.1.3. The Utterance Level

It is impressive to be able to type in a phonetic transcription of an utterance and have it spoken by a computer by joining the phonemes together. But real speech is not just a matter of joining segments together. You might be able to identify the words that are being spoken, but there is often a world of difference between the words that someone speaks and what he or she is actually *saying*. Emphasis, stress, and intonation are all essential features of real speech. They make the difference between speech being merely intelligible, and sounding *intelligent* in the sense that the speaker understands what he or she is talking about.

It is here that we begin to get into deep water. Somehow the computer must be told, or must find out, enough information about its utterances to say them intelligently. There are two possibilities. First, we could have a notation so that when you type in the phonetic transcription of an utterance, you could also communicate information about how it is to be said. Or second, you could have the computer decide for itself how things are to be said by making it "understand" what it is reading. Both of these approaches are discussed in Chapter 4.

Also, we need to consider some technical questions. Suppose, for example, we know what the intonation should be; that is, we know how the pitch of the voice should vary along the utterance. How are we to actually apply this varying pitch to the utterance? Suppose I give you a graph of pitch against time and ask you to map it onto a particular utterance. It is unlikely that the utterance will last for exactly the same length of time as the pitch graph. You could try squashing the pitch up or stretching it out so that it fits, but then it is unlikely that the result will sound right, for the prominent features of the intonation will probably miss the important syllables of the utterance. We need some way of taking a pitch graph and matching it up with an utterance by keying together the important parts of the graph with the important syllables of the utterance. This is what we look at first in Chapter 4.

Then we examine a method of describing and classifying artificial intonations in terms of their important features. The idea is that instead of measuring a graph of pitch against time from actual speech, we can construct the pitch artificially. It should be easy to specify the pitch so that, for example, when you type in a phonetic transcription of an utterance, you can type a number along with it that says what kind of intonation it will have. The computer program that generates the speech will need to have some knowledge of the kinds of intonation patterns used in natural speech, so that it will be able to fill in the details of the graph from the small amount of information—the classification number—you have given it.

Of course, it would be even nicer if the input to the system were plain text, instead of a phonetic transcription, and the computer program were clever enough to figure out what kind of intonation should be used. Chapter 4 discusses the problems with this approach and the sort of considerations that have to be taken into account. It doesn't really give definitive solutions—for there aren't any! Also, we look at the problems of pronunciation or how to make a phonetic transcription from plain English. Although this may be surprising, because the vagaries of English pronunciation are well-known, simple pronunciation schemes can work remarkably well. We look in detail at a particularly successful one.

1.1.4. The Application Level

In the final chapter, we examine applications of talking computers and the things you need to take into account to make successful speech systems. Suppose you have decided how to represent the speech inside the computer. You have written all the programs and purchased the hardware needed to generate the speech waveform. You have recorded the utterances you need, or made the word dictionary, or constructed the phoneme table, or whatever is needed for the particular method chosen. Now you can make the computer say any utterance you need. Suppose also that it sounds pretty good (quite a large assumption). What is there left to do?

Well, you probably want a system that people can interact with, rather than just a computer that says things that you tell it to. To build this system, you need to take account of the special nature of speech—that it is ephemeral. When a person using a word processor is stuck and doesn't remember what to do, he or she can sit and look at the screen and think. But that isn't so easy with speech. It's as if the screen goes away as soon as it has been displayed. You obviously need to take account of this and to provide such things as easy-to-use "repeat" facilities when the system is built. Also, the interface device will very likely be a telephone. In the absence of speech recognition, the keys on the touchtone phone are the only way to communicate things to the computer. Special care needs to be taken with the dialogue to make it easy for the user to pose queries using such a limited-input device.

We will also look at some actual systems that use speech output. Chapter 5 describes a talking calculator, a scheme for generating wiring instructions using a synthetic voice, speech output in the telephone exchange, and a talking and listening travel-consultant computer. These systems all use rather simple forms of speech output and have quite restricted vocabularies. Also described are more sophisticated systems: a telephone enquiry service that allows you to find out a variety of things from a computer over the telephone and a reading machine for the blind.

1.2. THE ANATOMY OF SPEECH

People speak by using their vocal cords as a sound source. This basic sound is then modified by resonances in the vocal tract. Although the most important part of the vocal tract is the mouth, the upper section of the throat is involved as well, as is the nasal cavity for certain sounds. The shape of the vocal tract is changed during speech by rapid gestures of the articulatory organs—the tongue, lips, jaw, and so on. These alter the frequencies of the resonances to give the different sounds that we know as the vowels and consonants of ordinary language.

What do you need to learn about this process for the purposes of making computers talk? That depends critically upon how speech is represented in the system. If utterances are stored as time waveforms—we look at this in the next chapter—the structure of speech is not important. With more interesting and flexible representations, however, you need to know something about the acoustic properties of the speech waveform. If you want to generate speech directly from plain text, you will have to learn quite a lot about linguistics—and you will still be disappointed that more isn't known about how people choose to say things the way they do.

The so-called *voiced* sounds of speech—like the sound you make when you say "aaah"—are produced by passing air up from the lungs through the larynx or voicebox, which is situated just behind the Adam's apple. The vocal tract from larynx to lips acts as a resonant cavity, magnifying certain frequencies and diminishing others.

The waveform generated by the larynx, however, is not simply a regular, smooth, oscillation like that in Figure 1.1(a). The larynx contains two folds of skin—the vocal cords—which blow apart and flap together again for each cycle of pitch. This makes a kind of triangular waveform like the one shown in Figure 1.1(b). The frequency of repetition of this waveform is the pitch of the voice. It is measured in cycles per second, called hertz. For a deep male voice, the pitch may go as low as 50 Hz, or fifty cycles per second. For high-pitched speech sounds it might reach 250 Hz. A typical median value of 100 Hz is shown in Figure 1.1. For a female voice the range is higher, up to about 500 Hz in speech. Singing can go much higher: A high C sung by a soprano has a frequency of just over 1000 Hz, and some opera singers can reach substantially higher than this.

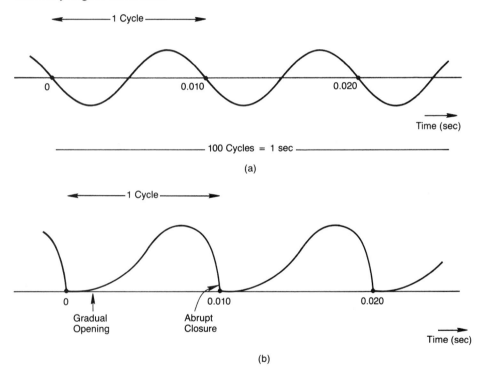

Figure 1.1 (a) Regular, smooth, waveform oscillating at 100 Hz (b) Waveform generated by the larynx.

The waveform of Figure 1.1(b), produced by the flapping action of the vocal cords, has a rich spectrum of harmonics or overtones. For example, with a pitch of 100 Hz there will be harmonics at 200 Hz, 300 Hz, 400 Hz, and so on. These harmonics get progressively less prominent as their frequency becomes higher. By 3200 Hz, or 3.2 kHz (kilohertz), which is five octaves above the fundamental frequency of 100 Hz, the harmonics are a thousand

times smaller than the fundamental. Each harmonic is affected by the resonances of the vocal tract.

1.2.1. Vocal Tract Resonances
A simple model of the vocal tract is just
a straight cylindrical tube, like an organ pipe, as shown in Figure 1.2. It has a
sound source at one end, the larynx, and is open at the other, the lips. You
may remember from your school physics courses that if L is the length of the
tube, the resonances have wavelengths of $4L$, $4L/3$, $4L/5$, ... These resonances are shown in the figure. Frequency times wavelength is speed, so if c is
the speed of sound in air, the resonant frequency of a wave of length $4L$ is
$c/4L$ times a second, or Hz. Similarly, the other resonances are at $3c/4L$,
$5c/4L$, ... Hz. For a male speaker, a typical distance from larynx to lips is
$L = 17$ cm. Using a figure of $c = 340$ m/s for the speed of sound, you can
calculate the resonant frequencies to be approximately 500 Hz, 1500 Hz,
2500 Hz, ...

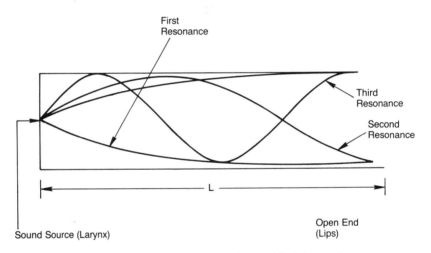

Figure 1.2 Resonances in the organ-pipe model of the vocal tract.

Now these are only *resonances,* not sound sources. To hear them, the
tube has to be excited by a sound source. The effect of each resonance is to
amplify the harmonics of the source which lie near it. Fortunately, as we have
seen, the waveform generated by the larynx has a rich spectrum of harmonics.
When excited by this waveform, the vocal tract resonances produce peaks
known as *formants* in the energy spectrum of the speech wave. These are
shown diagrammatically in Figure 1.3. The lowest formant, called *formant one,*
varies from around 200 Hz to 1000 Hz during speech. The exact range depends
on the size of the vocal tract. Formant two varies from around 500 to
2500 Hz, and formant three from around 1500 to 3500 Hz. Thus the crude

calculations above give a surprisingly good approximation to frequencies around the middle of the ranges.

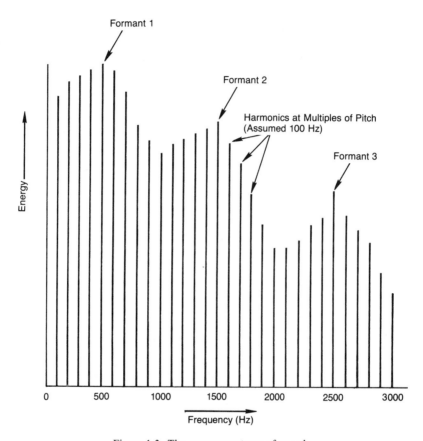

Figure 1.3 The energy spectrum of speech.

You can easily hear the lowest formant by whispering the vowels in the words "heed," "hid," "head," "had," "hod," "hawed," and "who'd." They appear to have a steadily descending pitch, yet since you are whispering there is no fundamental frequency. What you hear is the lowest resonance of the vocal tract—formant one. Some masochistic people can play simple tunes with this formant by putting their mouth in successive vowel shapes and knocking the top of their head with their knuckles—hard!

Of course, your mouth doesn't stand still in speech. The organ-pipe model describes the sound spectrum during a continuously held vowel with the mouth in a neutral position such as for "aaah." But in real speech the tongue and lips are in continuous motion. This alters the shape of the vocal tract, and by doing so changes the positions of the resonances. It is as if the organ pipe were being squeezed and expanded in different places all the time. Say *ee* as in "heed" and feel how close your tongue is to the roof of your mouth, causing a constriction near the front of the vocal cavity. Now say *ee—aa—ee* and feel the tongue moving up and down.

You can use a special frequency analyzer called a *sound spectrograph* to make a three-dimensional plot of the variation of the speech energy spectrum with time. Figure 1.4 shows a spectrogram of the utterance "go away." Frequency is given on the vertical axis, and bands are shown at the beginning to indicate the scale. Time is plotted horizontally, and energy is given by the darkness of any particular area. The lower few formants can be seen as dark bands extending horizontally, and they are in continuous motion. In the neutral first vowel of "away," the formant frequencies pass through approximately the 500 Hz, 1500 Hz, and 2500 Hz that we calculated earlier. In fact, formants two and three are somewhat lower than these values.

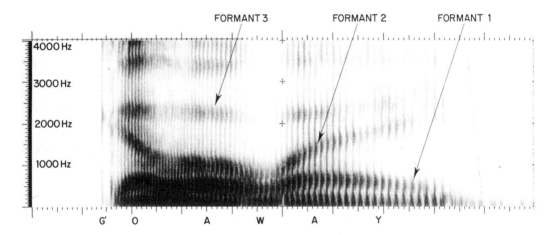

Figure 1.4 Spectrogram of utterance "go away." Courtesy of the Joint Speech Research Unit. © Crown Publishers 1980.

The fine vertical striations in the spectrogram correspond to single openings of the vocal cords, that is, to single pitch periods. Pitch changes continuously throughout an utterance. This can be seen on the spectrogram by the differences in spacing of the striations. Pitch change, or *intonation,* is singularly important in lending naturalness to speech.

On a spectrogram, a continuously held vowel shows up as a static energy spectrum. But beware—what we call a vowel in everyday language is not the same thing as a "vowel" in phonetic terms. Say "I" and feel how your tongue moves continuously while you're speaking. Technically, this is a *diphthong* or slide between two vowel positions, and not a single vowel. If you say *ar* as in "hard," and change slowly to *ee* as in "heed," you will make a diphthong not unlike that in "I." There are many more phonetically different vowel sounds than the a, e, i, o, and u that we normally think of. The words "hood" and "mood" have different vowels, for example, as do "head" and "mead." The principal acoustic difference between the various vowel sounds is in the frequencies of the first two formants.

A further complication is introduced by the nasal tract. This is a large cavity which is coupled to the oral tract by a passage at the back of the mouth. The passage is guarded by a flap of skin called the *velum*. You know about this because inadvertent opening of the velum during swallowing causes food or drink to go up your nose. The nasal cavity is switched in and out of the vocal tract by the velum during speech. It is used for the consonants m, n, and the ng sound in the word "singing." Vowels are frequently nasalized, too. A very effective demonstration of the amount of nasalization in ordinary speech can be obtained by cutting a nose-shaped hole in a large baffle which divides a room, speaking normally with your nose in the hole, and having someone listen on the other side. The frequency of occurrence of nasal sounds and the volume of sound that is emitted through the nose, are both surprisingly large. Interestingly enough, when we say in conversation that someone sounds "nasal," we often mean "non-nasal." When the nasal passages are blocked by a cold, nasal sounds are missing—ns turn into ds, and ms to bs.

When the nasal cavity is switched into the vocal tract, it introduces formant resonances, just as the oral cavity does. Although we can't alter the shape of the nasal tract significantly, the nasal formant pattern is not fixed, because the oral tract does play a part in nasal resonances. If you say m, n, and ng continuously, you can hear the difference and feel how it is produced by altering the combined nasal/oral tract resonances with your tongue position. The nasal cavity operates in parallel with the oral one.

1.2.2. Sound Sources

Speech involves sounds other than those caused by regular vibration of the larynx. When you whisper, the folds of the larynx are held slightly apart so that the air passing between them becomes turbulent. This makes a hissy sound, but you can't hear it directly because it must pass up through the vocal tract before it emerges from the lips. The formant peaks are still present, superimposed on the noise. Such sounds are called *aspirated,* and occur in the h of "hello," and for a very short time after the lips are opened at the beginning of "pit."

Constrictions made in the mouth produce hissy noises such as s, sh, and f. For example, in s the tip of the tongue is high up, very close to the roof of the mouth. Turbulent air passing through this constriction causes a random noise excitation, known as *frication*. Actually, the roof of the mouth is quite a complicated object. You can feel with your tongue a bony hump or ridge just behind the front teeth, and it is this that forms a constriction with the tongue for s. In sh, the tongue is flattened close to the roof of the mouth slightly farther back, in a position rather similar to that for ee but with a narrower constriction, while f is produced with the upper teeth and lower lip. Because they are made near the front of the mouth, the resonances of the vocal tract have little effect on these fricative sounds.

To distinguish them from aspiration and frication, the ordinary speech sounds like "aaah" which have their source in larynx vibration are known technically as *voiced*. Aspirated and fricative sounds are called *unvoiced*. Thus the three different sound types can be classified as

- voiced

- unvoiced (fricative)

- unvoiced (aspirated)

Can any of these three types occur together? It would seem that voicing and aspiration cannot, for voicing requires the larynx to be vibrating regularly, but for aspiration it must be generating turbulent noise. However, there is a condition known technically as *breathy voice* which occurs when the vocal cords are slightly apart, still vibrating, but with a large volume of air passing between to create turbulence. Voicing can easily occur in conjunction with frication. Corresponding to *s*, *sh*, and *f* we get the *voiced* fricatives *z*, the sound in the middle of words like "vision" which I will call *zh*, and *v*. A simple illustration of voicing is to say "ffffvvvvffff . . . ." During the voiced part you can feel the larynx vibrations with a finger on your Adam's apple, and it can be heard quite clearly if you stop up your ears. Technically, there is nothing to prevent frication and aspiration from occurring together—they do, for example, when a voiced fricative is whispered—but the combination is not an important one.

The complicated acoustic effects of noisy excitations in speech can be seen in the spectrogram in Figure 1.5 of "high altitude jets whizz past screaming."

1.2.3. The Source-Filter Model of Speech Production   We have seen that speech is produced by a sound source, whether voiced or unvoiced, being modified by the resonances of the vocal tract. This view is used extensively in speech synthesis and is known as the *source-filter model* of speech production. It allows the effect of the resonances to be modeled as a frequency-selective filter, operating on an input which is the waveform produced by the sound source. In other words, the frequency spectrum of the source is modified by multiplying it by the frequency characteristic of the filter. This can be seen in Figure 1.6, which shows a source spectrum and filter characteristic which combine to give the overall spectrum of Figure 1.3.

I mentioned above that the various fricatives are not modified by the resonances of the vocal tract to the same extent that voiced and aspirated sounds are. But they can still be modeled as a noise source followed by a filter to give them their different sound qualities.

One very interesting effect of the source-filter model is to separate the pitch and amplitude of the voice, which are largely properties of the source, from the articulation of the words by tongue and lip movements. Pitch and amplitude

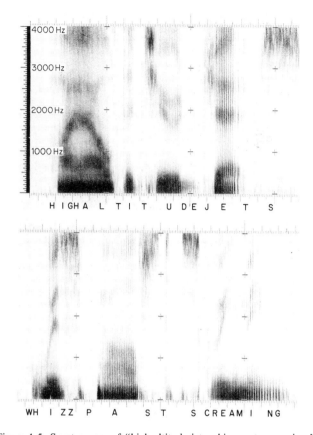

Figure 1.5 Spectrogram of "high-altitude jets whizz past screaming."

are called *prosodic* features, because they apply in a global manner to the utterance as a whole. In contrast, things which have to do with the articulation of the vowels and consonants are called *segmental,* because they operate on individual segments of the speech. The source-filter model separates the overall prosody from the actual segmental content of an utterance. This means that a human utterance can be recorded initially and then spoken by a machine with a variety of different intonations.

1.3. THE SOUNDS OF SPEECH

For some kinds of speech synthesis, we will need to identify and classify the individual sound segments. There is a real difficulty here because speech is by nature continuous and classifications are discrete. It is worth remembering this

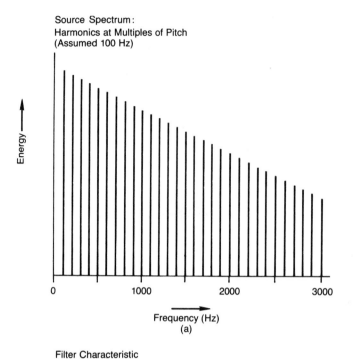

Source Spectrum:
Harmonics at Multiples of Pitch
(Assumed 100 Hz)

Energy ——▶

0   1000   2000   3000

Frequency (Hz)
(a)

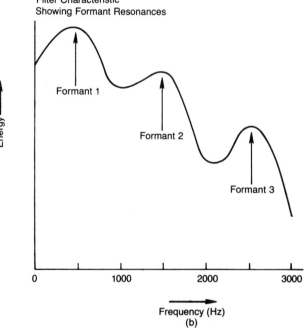

Filter Characteristic
Showing Formant Resonances

Energy ——▶

Formant 1

Formant 2

Formant 3

0   1000   2000   3000

Frequency (Hz)
(b)

Figure 1.6 The source-filter model: a source spectrum and filter characteristic.

difficulty, because it is all too easy to criticize the complex and often confusing attempts of linguists at classification.

Linguists call a written representation of the *sounds* of an utterance a *phonetic transcription* of it. The same utterance can be transcribed at different levels of detail. Simple transcriptions are called *broad* and more specific ones are called *narrow*. The broadest kind of transcription, and the most common, uses units termed *phonemes*.

1.3.1. The Phonemes of English   Linguists use an assortment of English letters, foreign letters, and special symbols to represent phonemes. In this book we use one- or two-letter codes, partly because they are more mnemonic and partly because they are more suitable for communication to computers. They are a direct transliteration of the standard International Phonetic Association symbols which are used by linguists.

TABLE 1.1   THE PHONEMES OF BRITISH ENGLISH

vowels		consonants			
uh	(the)	*p*	*t*	*k*	
a	(bud)	*b*	*d*	*g*	
e	(head)	*m*	*n*	*ng*	
i	(hid)				
o	(hod)	*r*	*w*	*l*	*y*
u	(hood)				
aa	(had)	*s*	*z*		
ee	(heed)	*sh*	*zh*		
er	(heard)	*f*	*v*		
uu	(food)	*th*	*dh*		
ar	(hard)	*ch*	*j*		
aw	(hoard)	*h*			

The classification of speech sounds into phonemes depends on the language being considered. Table 1.1 shows the phonemes of British English. The only difference between this and American English is in the vowel sounds. However, other languages can have radically different phonemes. In Japanese, for example, the sounds *r* and *l* actually correspond to the same phoneme. The Japanese language does not distinguish *r* from *l*. Japanese people *do not hear* the difference between "lice" and "rice." Although this may be hard to believe, there are sounds that are just as different as *r* and *l* that *you* do not distinguish. Take the words "key" and "caw," for example. Despite the difference in spelling, both of them begin with a *k* sound that corresponds, in English, to the same phoneme, called *k*. However, say them two or three times each, concentrating on the position of the tongue during the *k*. It is quite different in each case. For "key" it is raised, close to the roof of the mouth, in preparation for the *ee*, whereas in "caw" it is much lower down. The sound of the *k* is actually quite different in the two cases. Yet they correspond to the same phoneme, for there is no pair of words which relies on this difference to distinguish them—"key" and "caw" are obviously distinguished by their vowels, not by the initial consonant. You will find it hard to hear the difference between the two *k*s, precisely because they belong to the same phoneme and so the difference is not important for English. But experiment with a friend for a while, using very short *k*s of the two kinds, and you will probably become convinced of the difference. Another example is initial *h*s in the Cockney dialect of London, England. Cockneys do not hear, except with a special effort, the difference between "has" and "as," or "haitch" and "aitch," for the Cockney dialect does not recognize initial *h*s.

It is important to realize that there is not such a simple correspondence between sounds and phonemes as you might think. A speech synthesis system, emulating a person, should make the difference between the two *k* sounds, using the appropriate one in the appropriate context. Otherwise the speech will sound unnatural. If you give it only the phonetic transcription of the utterance, it will have to infer which *k* to use on the basis of its neighboring phoneme—just as you do, unconsciously.

Let's look at the phonemes in the list of Table 1.1, and at the more detailed breakdown of phoneme types given in Table 1.2. There is an everyday distinction between vowels and consonants. A vowel forms the center of every syllable, and one or more consonants may optionally surround the vowel. But the distinction sometimes becomes a little ambiguous. You often say a syllable like *sh* on its own, and it certainly does not contain a vowel. Furthermore, when people say "vowel" in everyday language, they are usually referring to the *written* vowels *a*, *e*, *i*, *o*, and *u*. There are many more vowel sounds. A vowel in written language is different from a vowel as a phoneme.

TABLE 1.2 PHONEME CATEGORIES

vowel	*uh a e i o u aa ee er uu ar aw*
diphthong	[not classified as individual phonemes]
glide	*r w l y*
stop	
unvoiced	*p t k*
voiced	*b d g*
nasal	*m n ng*
fricative	
unvoiced	*s sh f th*
voiced	*z zh v dh*
affricate	
unvoiced	*ch*
voiced	*j*
aspirate	*h*

Table 1.1 gives example words which contain the twelve phonetic vowels of English. One rather peculiar vowel is *uh*, which corresponds to the first vowel in the word "above." This is the sound produced by the vocal tract in a relaxed, neutral position. It never occurs in prominent, stressed syllables. The vowels later in the list are almost always longer than the earlier ones. In fact, the first six (*uh*, *a*, *e*, *i*, *o*, *u*) are often called *short* vowels, and the last five (*ee*, *er*, *uu*, *ar*, *aw*) *long* ones. The shortness or longness of the one in the middle (*aa*) is rather ambiguous.

We discussed diphthongs earlier. They are sequences of vowels, like "I," letter "a," and "ear." Many phoneticians classify diphthongs as separate phonemes. There are quite a few of them in English: "hay," "hoe," "high," "how," "boy," "hear," "hair," and "tour." You can approximate them by the sequences of vowels from Tables 1.1 and 1.2. For example, "I" becomes *aa i* or *ar i*, "a" becomes *e i*, and "ear" becomes *i uh* or *i er*. Such an approximation is certainly not exact, and this is underlined by the fact that I have had to give more than one sequence for "I" and "ear." But we will use it in this book.

The remaining phonemes are consonants. Table 1.2 shows that there are several categories of consonant: glides, stops, nasals, fricatives, affricates, and aspirates.

The glides are quite similar to vowels and diphthongs. They are voiced, continuous sounds, and you can say them and prolong them. The glide *r* is interesting because it can be realized acoustically in very different ways. Some people curl the tip of the tongue back—a so-called retroflex action of the tongue. Many people can't do this, and their *r*s sound like *w*s. The stage Scotsman's *r* is a trill where the tip of the tongue vibrates against the roof of the mouth. The phoneme *l* is also slightly unusual, for it is the only English sound which is "lateral"—air passes either side of the tongue, in two separate passages. Welsh has another lateral sound, a fricative, which is written "ll" as in "Llandudno."

The next category is the stops. These are formed by stopping up your mouth, so that air pressure builds up behind your lips, and releasing this pressure suddenly. The result is a little explosion—the stops are sometimes called *plosives*—which usually creates a very short burst of fricative noise. In some cases aspiration is present as well. Stops are further subdivided into voiced and unvoiced ones, depending upon whether voicing starts as soon as the plosion occurs or well after it. If you put your hand in front of your mouth when saying "pit," you can easily feel the puff of air that signals the plosion on the *p* and probably on the *t* as well.

In a sense, nasals are really stops as well, for the oral tract is blocked, although the nasal one is not. In fact, they are often called stops. In this book, *ng* refers to the sound in the middle and at the end of "singing." This is certainly not an *n* sound followed by a *g* sound, although it is true that in some English accents, "singing" is spoken with the *ng* followed by a *g* at each of its two occurrences. This particular nasal sound is peculiar because it never occurs at the beginning of a word in English. It does in other languages, however. For example, in Chinese the sound *ng* is a word in its own right and is a common family name.

For stops and nasals, there is a similarity in the *vertical* direction of Table 1.2, among *p*, *b*, and *m*; *t*, *d*, and *n*; and *k*, *g*, and *ng*. The stop *p* is an unvoiced version of *b*. Try saying them one after another. The nasal *m* is a nasalized version of *b*. After all, *b* is what you get if you try to say *m* when your nasal passage is blocked up because you have a cold. These three sounds are all made at the front of the mouth; while *t*, *d*, and *n*, which bear the same resemblance to each other, are made in the middle; and *k*, *g*, and *ng* are made at the back.

The unvoiced fricatives are quite straightforward, except perhaps for *th*, which is the sound at the beginning of "thigh." They are paired with the voiced fricatives on the basis of where in the mouth they are produced. For example, the voiced version of *th* is the *dh* at the beginning of "thy." When you say these two sounds you can probably feel that there is a lot of similarity between them—you don't have to move your tongue at all. The voiced fricative *zh* is a fairly rare phoneme, which is heard in the middle of "vision." It is the voiced version of the much more common *sh* in the middle of "fission."

Affricates are similar to fricatives but begin with a stopped sound. For example, the *ch* at the beginning of "chin" is very like the sequence *t sh*. You can compare the phrases "why choose" and "white shoes." The main difference is actually between the lengths of the vowels in "why" and "white," rather than in the actual sounds themselves. There is some controversy amongst linguists as to whether affricates should be considered as single phonemes or as sequences of stop phonemes and fricatives.

Finally comes the lonely aspirate, *h*. Aspiration does occur elsewhere in speech, particularly during the plosive burst of unvoiced stops.

1.3.2. Narrow Phonetic Transcription
The classification into phonemes is based upon a clear rationale for distinguishing between sounds according to how they affect meaning. For example, the different *k* sounds in "key" and "caw" are treated as the same phoneme, because the difference does not serve to distinguish any words of English. In Japanese, *r* and *l* would actually be the same phoneme, although they are obviously different for English. This classification is a "broad" one.

Narrower transcriptions are not so systematic. They use units called *allophones*. "Phone" is a more old-fashioned term for the same thing, and the misused word "phoneme" is often mistakenly employed where allophone is meant. Each phoneme has several allophones, more for a narrow transcription and less for a broad one. The allophones are different acoustic realizations of the same abstract unit. For example, the *k*s in "key" and "caw" may be considered as different allophones. Although we will not use symbols for allophones here, they are often indicated by little marks in a text which modify the basic phoneme classes. For example, a tilde (˜) over a vowel means that it is nasalized. A small circle underneath a consonant means that it is devoiced, as, for example, the *r* in "pray" is often devoiced.

Allophonic variation in speech occurs because of a mechanism called *coarticulation,* where a sound is affected by those that come either side of it. "Key"—"caw" is a clear example of this. The tongue position in the *k* anticipates that of the following vowel—high in the first case, low in the second. Coarticulation can be predicted by rules which try to show how a particular phonemic sequence will be realized by allophones. Such rules have been studied extensively by linguists.

The reason for coarticulation, and for the existence of allophones, lies in the physical constraints imposed by the motion of the tongue, jaw, and lips—particularly their acceleration and deceleration. An immensely crude model is as follows. The brain decides what phonemes to say. It then takes this sequence and translates it into neural commands, which actually move the tongue, jaw, and lips into target positions. However, other commands may be issued and executed before these targets are reached, and this accounts for coarticulation effects. Phonological rules for converting a phonemic sequence to an allophonic one are a sort of discrete model of the process. Particularly for work involving computers, it is possible that this rule-based approach will be overtaken by potentially more accurate methods which attempt to model the continuous articulatory motions directly.

1.4. PROSODY

When talking earlier about the utterance level of speech synthesis, I pointed out that to speak is much more than just to join together segments like words, phonemes, or allophones. Emphasis, stress, intonation, and tone of voice can all play important roles in communicating meaning. You might say that speech is somehow more than the sum of its parts, the parts being the sequence of phonemes which determines what words are said. But this is not quite accurate. The point is that some of the parts are those features of emphasis, stress, intonation, tone of voice, and so on, which have their effect on a grander scale than individual phonemes. To make computers talk properly, we will have to consider these different kinds of features as well as the words and phonemes.

Think of the computers and robots which you have seen simulated in science fiction films. Some of them—Hal in *2001,* C3PO in *Star Wars*—sound just like people. Others, like C3PO's friend R2D2, cannot speak at all, but make peculiar noises that are supposed to be understood by other characters in the story. Still others, notably the Daleks in *Doctor Who*, are quite understandable but speak in a grating monotone, lacking all emotion. You might call it "inhuman." These last illustrate what speech will sound like if you pay attention only to the stream of phonemes and ignore the higher-level effects. They represent the layman's stereotype of computer talk, a caricature of living speech—abrupt, arhythmic, and in a grating monotone—which was well characterized by Isaac Asimov when he wrote of speaking "all in capital letters."

The global features that ride on top of the phoneme stream are called *prosodic* features. Some people call them "suprasegmental" instead, to emphasize that they operate at a higher level than individual phoneme or syllable segments. A dictionary definition of prosody is the "science of versification, laws of meter." This emphasizes the aspects of stress and rhythm that are central to classical verse. There are, however, many other features which are more or less global. We will call them all *prosodic.*

Prosodic features can be split into two basic categories: features of voice quality and features of voice dynamics. Variations in voice quality are caused by anatomical differences and long-term muscular idiosyncrasies. For example, you speak differently when you have a sore throat or when you forget to put in your false teeth, and these are variations in voice quality. Such features have little part to play in current and projected applications for talking computers.

Variations in voice dynamics occur in three dimensions: pitch or fundamental frequency of the voice, time, and amplitude. In voiced speech, the pitch is the frequency of vibration of the vocal folds, shown as 100 Hz in Figure 1.1(b). For unvoiced sounds such as *s* and *sh*, there is no pitch. When you are singing, it is the pitch that makes the tune. Don't forget that speech has all sorts of other frequency components. A range from a low value right up to 4000 Hz is shown in the spectrograms of Figures 1.4 and 1.5. The pitch is the lowest component, and all other components are harmonics of it, as illustrated in Figure 1.6. The pattern of pitch variation within an utterance is called the *intonation.* This can be distinguished from the overall range within which that variation occurs. For example, you can use the same intonation pattern with a wider pitch range than usual for dramatic effect.

Intonation has a big effect on meaning. Pitch often—but by no means always—rises on a yes-no question, the extent and abruptness of the rise depending on features like whether a genuine information-bearing reply or merely confirmation is expected. You use a distinctive pitch pattern to introduce a new topic. Intonation can be used to bring out contrasts, as in

"He didn't have a *red* car, he had a *black* one."

In general, the intonation pattern you use depends not only on the text itself but on your interpretation of it and also on how you expect you listener to react to it. For example:

"He had a *red* car" (I think you thought it was black).
"He had a red *car*" (I think you thought it was a truck).

Let's move now to the time dimension. This encompasses the rhythm of the speech, pauses in it, and its overall tempo—whether it is uttered quickly or slowly. Variations in rhythm help to distinguish nouns from verbs, like *ex*tract from ex*tract*, and adjectives from verbs, like ap*prox*imate from approxi*mate*. Of course, other features play a part here too. For example, the vowel qualities differ in each pair of words. Nevertheless, if in a real conversation you distorted the timing so that the wrong syllable was short and the others long in these examples, your listener would very likely wonder what you actually said.

The third dimension, amplitude, is of relatively minor importance. You probably think that you stress words by making them louder, but that is actually not very often true. In fact, intonation and rhythm work together to produce the effect which is commonly called *stress*. We will return to this and discuss algorithms for synthesizing intonation and rhythm in Chapter 4.

Prosodic features have a very important role to play in communicating meaning. They are not fancy, optional components. They are certainly very difficult to deal with, largely because linguists do not yet know enough about them. But it is worthwhile trying to do something about the prosodic features of artificial speech. Otherwise, the stereotype outlined above of talking computers which sound like imbeciles will be perpetuated.

1.5. FURTHER READING

Brown, G., K.L. Currie, and J. Kenworthy, *Questions of Intonation.* London, England: Croom Helm, 1980. This book presents an intensive study of the prosodics of colloquial, living speech, with particular reference to intonation. Although not terribly relevant to talking computers, it gives great insight into how conversational speech differs from reading aloud.

Fry, D.B., *The Physics of Speech.* Cambridge, England: Cambridge University Press, 1979. A simple and readable account of speech science, this book includes a good and completely nonmathematical introduction to frequency analysis.

Ladefoged, P., *A Course in Phonetics.* New York: Harcourt Brace and Johanovich, 1975. Usually books entitled "A course on . . ." are dreadfully dull, but this is a wonderful exception. An exciting, readable, almost racy introduction to phonetics, full of little experiments you can try yourself.

O'Connor, J.D., *Phonetics.* London, England: Penguin, 1973. This is another introductory book on phonetics. It is packed with information on all aspects of the subject.

Witten, I.H., *Principles of Computer Speech.* London, England: Academic Press, 1982. This book contains all the information in the present book, and a lot more besides. But it has a much more academic presentation and gets significantly involved in the mathematics of speech analysis and synthesis. Read it when you have finished the present book, if you want more details and theory.

2

The Signal Level: Generating Speech Waveforms

At the lowest level in a speech synthesis system is the hardware device that actually produces the speech waveform and sends it to an amplifier and loudspeaker. It operates under computer control. The computer may be a microcomputer chip in a talking calculator or hand-held toy, or a large mainframe in a research laboratory. It supplies the hardware with information which describes, in some suitable form, the waveform that is supposed to be produced. Because this speech waveform is continually changing, information will have to be supplied continually.

The hardware device that you use to generate the speech waveform is often called a *speech synthesizer*, although this is perhaps a bad name. "Synthesis" means "the combining of elements or parts or ingredients into a system or whole." Usually, the controlling computer does quite a lot of the combining, and sometimes virtually all of it. To talk of the hardware itself as the synthesizer can be a bit misleading, although the term is by now so entrenched that I will continue to use it in this book.

This chapter is about generating the speech waveform. We will look at several quite different types of synthesizer hardware. In order to keep things on a practical level, actual commercial products are described in some detail to illustrate the principles that are used. I have chosen to illustrate different methods of synthesis by looking at a few trail-blazing products that changed the course of the subject. These are not necessarily recommended for actual use: an appendix to this book surveys current market offerings to give an idea of what is available commercially.

You may be surprised to hear that there is quite a lot of theory behind the design of speech-output devices. Being interested more in *using* them rather than *designing* them, we will not tackle this theory. Instead, we look hard at the nuts and bolts of how you actually drive the commercial devices from your computer—what information they need, how often it has to be supplied, and what encoding methods are used to reduce the data.

When thinking about generating speech artificially, you should always bear in mind that your ordinary domestic cassette tape recorder is man-made and talks. Is it a speech synthesizer? It all depends on what you mean by synthesis. It certainly has a great deal in common with some other devices that are usually called synthesizers. Of course, it doesn't operate under computer control, but it could—you have probably seen cassette recorders attached to home computers.

The tape recorder has many advantages over other kinds of speaking machines. Very cheap, it can produce speech which is perfectly natural-sounding and of extremely high quality compared with the other methods discussed in this book. It is equally good with male, female, or children's voices. Recording is just as cheap as replay. So why all the fuss about computer speech?

Well, look at what is wrong with the tape recorder. For one thing, it is difficult to replay utterances in an order different from that in which they were recorded. Random-access tape recorders can be built, typically using a second track on the tape as an index track, with tones that indicate where new utterances begin. Of course, this makes them much more expensive. Also they often break down because whenever the tape starts and stops, stresses are placed on the mechanism.

Rapid-access "tape recorders" can easily be made by a variety of means — rotating analog drums instead of tape, digital computer disks, or even "solid-state" integrated circuit technology. This makes them more expensive than domestic cassette recorders, but computer storage costs are continuing to drop dramatically. It also makes it somewhat more difficult to record on them, because additional computer equipment is needed. Still, it is worth reflecting on whether there are any other disadvantages to tape-recording techniques for computer output, apart from the difficulty of quick access.

There are. We will review them at the beginning of the next section. Despite this, however, many present-day voice response systems *do* store what amounts to a direct recording of the speech waveform. The next section describes how this is done using both analog and digital storage means. We will be more interested in digital storage because of its greater flexibility, higher reliability, and lower cost of rapid access to different utterances. The remaining sections of the chapter look at three more sophisticated methods of producing speech waveforms from stored data.

The first two methods, although technically quite different, are fairly similar from the point of view of someone who is writing computer programs to generate speech. They have to be supplied with data at a much lower rate than that corresponding to direct recording of the waveform—say a hundred times a second as opposed to many thousands of times a second. They work by using a "parametric" representation of the speech waveform. The speech is described in terms of quantities, called *parameters*, which vary much more slowly than the raw waveform itself. In the case of the first technique we look at, termed *linear prediction* and embodied in the Texas Instruments Speak 'n Spell toy, these parameters can be related to the shape of the vocal tract of a human speaker. Of course, this changes continually during speech due to tongue movements and so on. For the second, called *formant synthesis* and used by the Computalker speech synthesizer for hobby computers, the parameters represent the acoustic wave in a different way, through the positions of vocal tract resonances. However, the shape of the vocal tract and the frequencies of its resonances are obviously closely related to each other, so the synthesizers are not as different as they might seem at first sight.

The last device we will examine for making the waveform is a sound-segment synthesizer, illustrated by the popular Votrax product. This actually uses a similar formant synthesis method to Computalker internally, but looks so different to the user that we describe it separately. Votrax is not driven by parameters supplied a hundred times a second, but by a more direct representation of the speech in terms of phoneme-like sound segments. Actually, the sound segments operate at a rather lower level than phonemes, because contextual effects of one phoneme on another are not taken into account automatically but must be provided explicitly by the controlling computer as additional sound segments. Nevertheless, the technique is an extremely interesting one because it has the potential of taking some of the burden of phoneme-level synthesis off the computer and putting it directly in the synthesizer hardware.

2.1. DIRECT RECORDING

Before we dive into recording and replay techniques, let's first look at what is *wrong* with direct recording of the human voice for making computers talk.

In many applications of speech-output systems, you need to be able to build up utterances by joining together separately recorded parts. Suppose your system has to produce spoken telephone numbers, and you plan to have just one recording of each digit, and join together the appropriate ones when a number is to be spoken.

It is easy to imagine doing this with direct-recording techniques. You could get an idea of how it would sound by recording the digits on a tape recorder and cutting and splicing the tape. By using digital recordings, stored on computer disk, a splicing operation like this could easily be done automatically. But what would it sound like? How would you say the digits when you recorded them in the first place? You would probably pronounce each word in what is called *citation form*, as an utterance in its own right. For example, in the familiar "count-down" sequence, "nine ... eight ... seven ... six ...," the words are spoken in citation form. Now imagine the difference between this and the telephone number 987-6543, spoken normally. Try speaking the two versions out loud. When you say the phone number, you use a definite grouping of digits, three and then four, with a pause in between. (At least, you do if you are used to dealing with phone numbers in this format.) Furthermore, you use a different intonation pattern on digits in different positions. For example, the "7" will have a slightly rising pitch, indicating that the number is still incomplete; whereas the "3" will have a falling one to show that it is finished. The two ways of saying the number are so different that I bet if you asked me for my number, and I said it in "countdown" mode, you would reply "What?" and get me to repeat it. Try it with a friend.

Scientists have performed experiments which demonstrate this point. They have, for example, recorded separate words on an ordinary tape recorder, spliced the tape with the words in a different order to make sentences, and played the sentences to people who were scored on the number of key words which they identified correctly. Now with normal speech, putting a word into the context of a sentence increases the likelihood that it will be recognized, compared with when it is spoken by itself. This is because the extra context gives clues about the word. However, these experiments showed that embedding a word in a constructed sentence actually *decreases* the likelihood of recognition, because the intonation and rhythm sound unnatural. When the speech is uttered slowly, there is a considerable improvement in the results. This indicates that if listeners have more time to think about what they hear, they can overcome the lack of proper intonation and rhythm.

Nevertheless, direct recording is often used in present-day speech-output systems. Let's look at modern techniques of recording and replay.

2.1.1. Analog Recording   A tape recorder stores the speech in analog form, by changing the magnetization on the tape to match the speech waveform. As discussed above, using tape makes it difficult to replay the speech in a different order. However, if you store speech on a rotating magnetic drum instead of on tape, it is quite easy to switch to a different track on the drum at each revolution. For example, the IBM 7770 Audio Response Unit uses drums which rotate twice every second. Each drum has 32 tracks, and so can store 32 half-second words. On replay, you can switch between words in any order you want. If you want to record a word or phrase that is longer than half a second, you can split it between two adjacent tracks. Unfortunately, the fact that everything has to work in half-second units of time makes it virtually impossible to generate connected utterances by assembling together appropriate words.

The Cognitronics Speechmaker uses the same sort of idea, but records the analog speech waveform on photographic film instead of a magnetic drum. There is nothing new about storing audio waveforms optically. This is how soundtracks are recorded on ordinary movie films. Another example of optical storage is the original version of the "speaking clock," provided as a telephone service by the British Post Office in the middle 1930s. This used concentric tracks on flat glass discs to store waveforms. To synchronize the utterances. a clock pendulum, swinging four times a second, supplied current to an electric motor. This drove a shaft equipped with cams and gears that rotated three glass discs at appropriate speeds. These discs contained utterances for seconds, minutes, and hours. Needless to say, this is not the kind of technology that is used today.

2.1.2. Digitizing Speech

Nowadays, if prerecorded speech needs to be accessed with the words in a different order, it is invariably stored in digital form. This means that standard computer storage devices can be used, providing rapid access to any segment of the speech at relatively low cost. The economics of mass production means that random-access digital stores cost much less than random-access analog ones. This is because the market for computer storage is so large. Storing speech digitally lets us piggy-back on this market and take advantage of low prices. Furthermore, it reduces the amount of special equipment needed for speech output. You can buy very cheap speech input/output interfaces for standard home computers and use the storage devices provided on the computer for speech as well as programs and data. Another advantage of digital over analog recording is that electronic memory chips can be used for hand-held devices which need small quantities of speech. This saves the cost which is always associated with rotating mechanical stores.

When an analog waveform is converted to digital form, the result is a list of numbers which give its magnitude at successive points in time. Figure 2.1 shows the idea. A small time interval called the "sampling interval" is chosen first. At each successive sampling interval you look at the waveform and measure its height. The list of numbers that you get is the digital version of the analog waveform. The sampling operation is like taking a continuous stretch of time and marking discrete, equally spaced points on it, say a thousand times a second. At each sampling point, when you measure the height of the waveform, you do so with a certain accuracy—the accuracy of the ruler you are using. Both the sampling and the measurement operations introduce distortions into the signal, and it is important to appreciate their effects.

Figure 2.2 shows a real speech waveform, lasting for a total of about five seconds. The waveform for the first word, "the," is shown magnified and magnified again. The bottom waveform lasts for about 0.115 s, or 115 ms. A "ms," or "millisecond," is a thousandth of a second. It is fairly obvious that if you sample this a hundred times a second, so that there are only eleven or twelve samples in the bottom line, most of the information will be lost. On the other hand, sampling a million times a second, so that there are 115,000 samples for the bottom waveform, is probably much more than is necessary to preserve the characteristics of the signal. What is the "correct" sampling rate? A

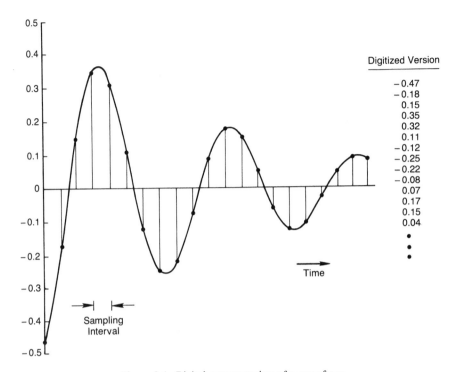

Digitized Version
−0.47
−0.18
0.15
0.35
0.32
0.11
−0.12
−0.25
−0.22
−0.08
0.07
0.17
0.15
0.04

Figure 2.1 Digital representation of a waveform.

basic theoretical result says that a signal can be reconstructed accurately from samples only if it does not contain components whose frequency is greater than half the frequency of sampling.

To illustrate this, Figure 2.3 shows two pure-tone waveforms with different frequencies, sampled at too low a rate. Imagine that you cannot see the waveforms themselves, but only the sample points. Then you will perceive absolutely no difference between the two, for the sampled values are identical for the two waveforms. Obviously the sample rate is too low to reflect the difference between them. In fact, it is slightly less than half the frequency of the second waveform. In Figure 2.4, however, you can see the effect of a rather higher sampling rate. Now the two sampled versions are definitely different. If you draw straight lines between the sample values in each case, you get rough approximations to the original waveforms. With a more sophisticated reconstruction method, you can regain the original waveforms from the sampled versions.

How does this apply to speech? Well, ordinary speech contains frequencies up to perhaps 8 or 12 kHz. "Hertz" means a cycle per second, so one kHz is 1000 cycles per second, and 12 kHz is 12,000 cycles per second. However,

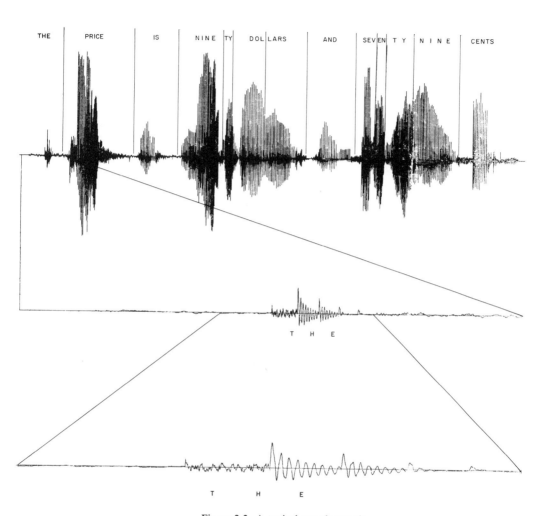

Figure 2.2 A typical speech waveform.

the high frequencies are not as important as the lower ones for understanding what is said. For example, consider telephone-quality speech. Telephones provide a familiar standard of speech quality which, although it can only be an approximate "standard," will be much used throughout this book. The telephone network aims to transmit only frequencies lower than 3.4 kHz. Actually, transmitting speech through the telephone system degrades its quality very significantly, probably more than you realize, since everyone is so accustomed to telephone speech. Try the dial-a-disc service and compare it with high-fidelity music for a striking example of the kind of degradation introduced by the telephone network.

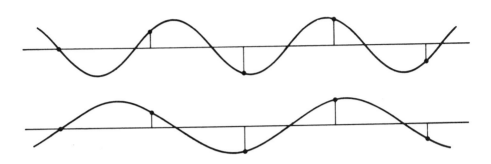

Figure 2.3 Two pure-tone waveforms, sampled at too low a rate.

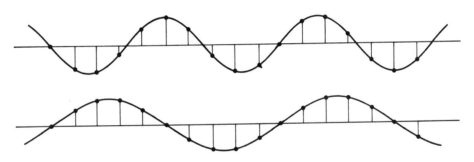

Figure 2.4 The same waveforms sampled at a higher rate.

For telephone-quality speech, the sampling frequency must be chosen to be at least twice 3.4 kHz, that is, 6.8 kHz. It is prudent to allow some latitude here, and so a sample rate of 8 kHz is commonly used. Of course, components at higher than half this frequency are actually present in a speech signal, and these must be removed by a "presampling filter" before the speech waveform is sampled.

Now that we have decided how fast to sample the speech, let's turn to how accurately the size of each sample value should be measured. Measurement is done by a device called an *A/D*, or "analog-to-digital," *converter*. This has as input the constant analog voltage produced by the sampler and gives as output a corresponding binary value. The simplest correspondence is *uniform* quantization, where the amplitude range is split into equal regions by points termed *quantization levels*, and the output is a binary representation of the nearest quantization level to the input voltage. Typically, for speech, 2048 quantization levels might be used. 2048 is an exact power of two, namely 2^{11}, so eleven bits of information would be needed to store each sample. If the speech signal is represented as a voltage which lies in the range $0 - 10$ V, then an input of $1 \times 10/2048 = 0.005$ V or less would give a binary output of 00000000000; an input of between 0.005 and 0.010 V would give an output of 00000000001; an input of between 4.995 and 5.000 V would give an output of 10000000000; and so on. In fact, the signal is usually first adjusted to have an average value of zero, so that half the levels correspond to negative input voltages and the other half to positive ones. However, this need not concern us here.

The use of 11-bit quantization implies a precision of $1/2048 = 0.05$ percent. At first sight, it is surprising that such a high precision is needed for adequate representation of speech signals. Experiments conducted by telephone engineers have shown that a signal-to-noise ratio of some $25 - 35$ dB (decibels) is enough to avoid undue harshness of quality, loss of intelligibility, and listener fatigue for speech at a comfortable level. This translates into an accuracy of around 3 percent. So the 0.05 percent accuracy of 11-bit quantization seems to be overdoing things quite a bit.

However, the noise level is relative to the maximum amplitude range of the conversion. Look at the very peaky nature of the typical speech waveform given in Figure 2.2. It is most important when you are digitizing it that the extreme levels of the conversion be far enough apart to avoid clipping. Clipping is shown in Figure 2.5, and will introduce a nasty high-frequency buzzing sound into the speech. Therefore, the maximum amplitude level of the A/D converter must be set very conservatively. This means that for most of the time, only a small fraction of the range of the converter is actually being used. Furthermore, different people speak at very different volumes, and the overall level fluctuates constantly with just one speaker. Experience shows that while 8- or 9-bit quantization may provide sufficient accuracy to preserve telephone-quality speech if the overall speaker levels are carefully controlled, about eleven bits are generally needed for a practical system. Even then it is useful if speakers are provided with an indication of the amplitude of their speech. A traffic-light indicator with red signifying clipping overload, orange a suitable level, and green too low a value is often convenient for this.

So far, we have been talking of *linear* quantization. However, the peakiness of the speech signal illustrated in Figure 2.2 makes you suspect that a nonlinear representation, for example a logarithmic one, could provide better accuracy over a wider range of input amplitudes. Figure 2.6 shows the quantization levels for a logarithmic representation. You can see that they are close together in the middle but more widely spaced towards the edges. This means that although the total range is big enough to prevent clipping, accuracy is still preserved for small signals by putting most of the quantization levels in the middle. The idea of nonlinearly quantizing a signal to achieve adequate accuracy over a wide variety of amplitudes is called *companding*, a contraction of "compressing-expanding." The original signal can be retrieved from a companded version by antilogarithmic expansion.

Figure 2.5 The effect of clipping on a speech wave.

Logarithmic encoders and decoders are available from many semiconductor manufacturers as single-chip devices called *codecs*, an abbreviation for "coder/decoder." Intended for use on digital communication links, these generally provide a serial output bit-stream, which should be converted to parallel by a shift register if the data is intended for a computer. Because of the potentially vast market for codecs in telecommunications (they will eventually appear in every telephone), they are made in great quantities and are consequently very cheap. Estimates of the speech quality necessary for telephone applications indicate that 7- or 8-bit accuracy is needed, using logarithmic encoding.

For digital storage of speech, we have seen that a sampling rate of around 8 kHz should be used, and that it is best to encode each sample in seven or eight bits by using the logarithmic method. This leads to a data rate of 56 or 64 Kbit/s. We will see later in this chapter that there are ways of reducing this data rate very substantially by using more sophisticated coding techniques. But first let us look at digital stores and what we can expect of them.

2.1.3. Digital Stores and Their Capacities   A computer-based speech storage system may need to hold a large number of audio messages. In many cases the storage should be relatively permanent, so that the speech messages come with the system and are not destroyed when power to the unit is switched off. Such storage is called ROM—*read-only memory*. Some method of entering the waveform into the store in the first place is necessary. With ordinary ROM this is done during manufacture. More convenient for product development is PROM—*programmable read-only memory*, which permits once-and-for-all

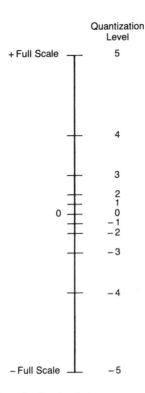

Figure 2.6   Quantization levels for logarithmic quantization.

programming after manufacture, and EPROM—*erasable programmable read-only memory*, which can be erased and reprogrammed as necessary.

Current commercial ROM chips can hold 32 Kbyte of information and cost a few dollars. One byte is eight bits, so 32 Kbyte is 256 thousand bits. Storing speech at 64 Kbit/s, a single ROM chip can therefore hold four seconds of speech. A card containing, say, eight ROM chips could hold a small fifty- or hundred-word vocabulary.

Of course, technology is changing all the time. Thirty-two Kbyte ROMs represent technology that is currently easily available commercially. At present, the record for ROM capacity is held by a chip designed to store Chinese characters. There are, as you may know, a very large number of Chinese characters. The chip was described in 1980 at the International Solid State Circuits Conference in San Francisco, and has a capacity of 4 Mbit (four million bits), or 500 Kbyte. This single chip is the equivalent of sixteen 32 Kbyte chips. A card containing, say, eight of these state-of-the-art ROMs has enough storage for around ten minutes of speech. Although this would probably provide an adequate vocabulary of words and phrases for many applications of talking computers, it still does not seem very much compared with a cassette tape recorder! There remains the problem of how to join together individual words and phrases to make them sound more natural, and we return to this in the next chapter.

With only very small storage volumes possible on ROM chips, it is no wonder that considerable effort has gone into representations of the speech waveform that are more economical than the 64 Kbit/s or so needed for straightforward digitized speech. We look at some of these in the following sections.

What about computer disks? Many applications of talking computers can't use disks, because it isn't possible to make them really portable. Being mechanical, they are inherently expensive and require more power than small batteries can provide. However, if the equipment doesn't have to be portable, disks can provide a much greater volume of storage than ROM chips.

Floppy disks, such as those used in most home computers and in many word processors, hold between 256 Kbyte and 2 Mbyte. Thus they have a rather larger capacity than the state-of-the-art ROM chips. But hard disks hold much more. Starting at 5 or 10 Mbyte, they commonly go up to 300 Mbyte. The 90-minute capacity of a cassette tape is reached by a 43-Mbyte disk, using straightforward digitized speech at 64 Kbit/s. Of course, the cost of such a disk unit, at something like $10,000, exceeds that of a cassette tape recorder by three orders of magnitude. The use of videodisks—which will be common domestic items by the end of the decade—could increase the storage by a factor of 50 over ordinary disks and reduce the price as well.

2.2. LINEAR PREDICTIVE SYNTHESIZERS: THE SPEAK 'N SPELL TOY

It is possible to reduce the data storage requirements of speech from the 64 Kbit/s or so that is required for direct digitization to around 1 Kbit/s. Although some speech quality is inevitably sacrificed, intelligibility is still retained. Speech stored at lower data rates—down to 500 bit/s—has been demonstrated, but its low quality makes it unsuitable for use except in special (e.g., military) situations. Synthesis of speech from a textual representation, say from plain or somewhat embellished English, brings the data rate down much lower; we will be talking about this in subsequent chapters. However, for *stored* speech, where a particular human utterance is recorded and processed to reduce the data rate, 1 Kbit/s seems to be a practical lower limit.

This is approximately the data rate used in the Texas Instruments (TI) speech chip. Introduced in the summer of 1978, this was the first single-chip speech synthesizer. It was a remarkable development, combining recent advances in signal processing with the very latest in very-large-scale integrated-circuit technology. Packaged in the Speak 'n Spell toy photographed in

Figure 2.7, it was a striking demonstration of imagination and prowess in integrated electronics. It gave TI a long lead over its competitors and surprised many experts in the speech field. Overnight, it seemed, digital speech technology descended from research laboratories with their expensive and specialized equipment into a $50.00 consumer item. Naturally TI did not sell the chip separately but only as part of their mass-market product; nor would they make available information on how to drive it directly. (Such information could soon be had on the computer hobbies underground network.) Only recently when other similar devices appeared on the market did they unbundle the package and sell the chip.

Figure 2.7 The Speak 'n Spell toy.

The TI chip uses a method of synthesis called *linear prediction*, and we will have a look at how it works shortly. This provides speech of reasonable quality at a very low data rate. It is hard to quote the data rate of the chip exactly, because it depends on the exact detail of the waveform being stored, but the average rate is in the region of 1.2 Kbit/s. Speech researchers, incidentally, sometimes scoff at what they perceive to be the poor quality of the toy's speech; but considering the data rate used it is remarkably good. Anyway, I have never heard a child complain—although it is not uncommon to misunderstand a word. Two 16-Kbyte read-only memories are used in the toy to hold data for about 330 words and phrases—lasting between three and four minutes—of speech. At the time (mid-1978) these memories were the largest that were available in the industry. The data flow and user dialogue are handled by a microprocessor, which is the fourth large chip in the photograph of Figure 2.8.

Figure 2.8 Circuitry inside the Speak 'n Spell toy.

A schematic diagram of the toy is given in Figure 2.9. It has a small display which shows uppercase letters. Some teachers of spelling hold that the lack of lowercase destroys any educational value that the toy may have. It has a full 26-key alphanumeric keyboard with fourteen additional control keys. This is the toy's Achilles' heel, for the keys fall out after extended use. More recent toys from TI use an improved keyboard. The keyboard is laid out alphabetically instead of in QWERTY order, possibly missing an opportunity to teach kids to type as well as spell. An internal connector permits vocabulary expansion with up to fourteen more read-only memory chips. Controlling the toy is a small microprocessor. However, the synthesizer chip does not receive data from the processor. During speech, it accesses the memory directly and returns control to the processor only when an end-of-phrase marker is found in the data stream. Meanwhile the processor is idle and cannot even be interrupted from the keyboard. Moreover, in one mode of operation the toy embarks upon a long monologue and remains deaf to the keyboard—it cannot even be turned off. Any three-year-old will quickly discover that a sharp slap solves the problem. A useful feature is that the device switches itself off if unused for more than a few minutes.

2.2.1. Linear Predictive Parameters   Ordinary digitized speech has a high data rate because the waveform has to be sampled at a high rate. For example,

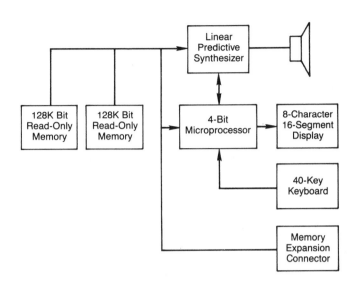

Figure 2.9 Block diagram of the Speak 'n Spell toy.

the 64-Kbit/s data rate for telephone-quality speech is generated by having to store 8-bit samples 8000 times a second. In order to reduce this substantially, we have to find a way of retaining sufficient information about the waveform which does not change so quickly as the waveform itself. Then it will not have to be sampled so fast.

Now this may seem impossible, for we have seen that to preserve a waveform you have to sample at twice the frequency of the highest component—which is around 3.4 kHz for telephone-quality speech. But look at it from a different point of view. You make speech by using your vocal tract and associated organs: larynx, tongue, jaw, lips. You certainly don't move them so fast that they have to be sampled 8000 times a second to reproduce the movements. Physical inertia reduces the time constants involved to something more like a tenth of a second. Perhaps we could take advantage of this to code the speech in an entirely different way, forgetting about the waveform and concentrating on how it is produced. This would lead to somehow measuring, or calculating, *parameters* of the speech which describe the vocal tract shape; and storing changes in these parameters at physiological rates rather than at speech waveform rates. Then a synthesis operation would be necessary on replay to reproduce the waveform from the stored parameters.

And this is exactly what the TI chip does. New parameter values are stored every 20 ms, or fifty times a second. This is over a hundred times slower than the 8 kHz sampling rate needed for the raw waveform. Of course, more than one number has to be stored every 20 msec and this loses some of the advantage that has been gained. In fact the TI chip uses quite fancy coding techniques to ensure that only those parameters that have changed significantly need to be stored. On average, it needs to store only 24 bits of information, 50 times a second; it is this that leads to the average data rate of 1.2 Kbit/s.

What are the parameters? Well, there are twelve of them. The first two, pitch and energy (loudness), are easy to understand. When a human utterance is encoded for the TI chip, the pitch and loudness are measured every 20 ms. It is quite easy to see that this is a high enough sampling rate for these parameters. You don't change the pitch of your voice very rapidly in speech, because to do so requires a significant vocal effort (ask an opera singer). Neither does the amplitude alter quickly.

The other ten parameters are actually related to the shape of the vocal tract. Figure 2.10 shows a diagram of the vocal tract. It turns out that the organ-pipe model of speech production, which we encountered in the last chapter, is quite a good one. You can ignore the physiological details of tongue, jaw, and lips, and visualize the tract as a "generalized cylinder." The cross-section is always round, but its area varies along the pipe. The pipe distorts and changes shape with time, of course; this is what makes the different sounds of speech. But it only changes shape at physiological rates. All we need to store is some information about the cross-sectional area at different points along the tube; we update this information regularly at a low rate.

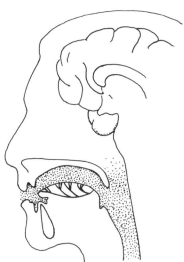

Figure 2.10 Cross section of your vocal tract.

In fact, a very crude quantization of the pipe is enough. The TI chip effectively divides it into just five sections and stores two numbers for each. This gives the ten parameters that are mentioned above. The cross-sectional area is not stored directly, but rather in the form of what are called *reflection coefficients*, which characterize the sonic reflections at the interfaces between each pair of sections. However, we need not worry about the details of exactly what they represent—it is enough to know that they somehow describe the vocal tract shape.

This raises the question of how you determine suitable values for the changing reflection coefficients for a stretch of speech. By now, you are probably imagining people taking measurements off an X-ray movie of a person speaking. Don't. It's not as bad as that. There are techniques for *linear predictive analysis* of a speech waveform to extract the parameters needed for linear predictive synthesis. While these techniques are not hard to mechanize in the form of computer programs, you need to do some fairly complicated mathematics to discover how they work. We won't consider them here. You need to know only that, given a recording of a human utterance, it is possible to analyze it into linear predictive parameters. In fact, there exist linear predictive coder-decoder systems which analyze utterances in real time, transmit the parameters over a low-bandwidth communication link, and resynthesize them immediately at the other end so that you can have a telephone conversation.

2.2.2. Driving the TI Chip
All of the control parameters for the TI chip are represented in 10-bit fixed-point form; that is, as numbers between 0 and 1023. As we have seen, there are twelve parameters for the device: ten reflection coefficients, energy, and pitch. These are updated every 20 ms. However, if 10-bit values were stored for each, a data rate of 120 bits every 20 ms, or 6 Kbit/s, would be needed. While this is well below the 64 Kbit/s rate needed for ordinary digitized speech, it is much more than the 1.2 Kbit/s actually attained by the TI chip. If no further encoding were used, the capacity of the two read-only memory chips would be reduced to well under a minute of speech—perhaps 65 words and phrases.

One very useful feature of the reflection coefficients which drive the TI chip is that the speech is not too sensitive to their precise values. Although the chip itself uses 10-bit quantities for each parameter, they are further encoded in the ROM memory which drives it. A nonlinear quantization scheme is used, where the parameter values in the ROM are interpreted through a quantization table to yield a 10-bit coefficient. In other words, a smaller stored value, say a 4-bit one, is used as an index to a table containing sixteen 10-bit numbers. The 4-bit value tells which 10-bit number to use as the actual parameter value.

Table 2.1 shows the number of bits devoted to each parameter. There are 4 bits for energy, and 5 bits for pitch and the first two reflection coefficients. Thereafter the number of bits allocated to reflection coefficients decreases steadily, for higher coefficients are less important for intelligibility than lower ones. With a 1-bit "repeat" flag, whose role is explained shortly, the frame size becomes 49 bits. Updated every 20 ms, this gives a data rate of just under 2.5 Kbit/s—or about twice the actual average data rate of 1.2 Kbit/s.

The parameters are expanded into 10-bit numbers by a separate quantization table for each one. For example, the five pitch bits address a 32-word

TABLE 2.1 BIT ALLOCATION FOR THE
SPEAK 'N SPELL CHIP

parameter	bits	
energy	4	Energy = 0 means 4-bit frame
pitch	5	
repeat flag	1	Repeat flag = 1 means 10-bit frame
k1	5	
k2	5	
k3	4	
k4	4	Pitch = 0 (unvoiced) means 28-bit frame
k5	4	
k6	4	
k7	4	
k8	3	
k9	3	
k10	3	Otherwise 49-bit frame
	49 bits	

look-up table which returns a 10-bit value. The transformation is logarithmic in this case, the lowest pitch being around 50 Hz and the highest 190 Hz.

The raw data rate of 2.5 Kbit/s is reduced to an average of 1.2 Kbit/s by further coding techniques. A full 49-bit frame is used only when absolutely necessary. In other cases, smaller frames are used as shown in the table. First, if the energy parameter is zero, the frame is silent, and no more parameters are transmitted. This gives a 4-bit frame. Second, if the "repeat" flag is 1, all reflection coefficients are held over from the previous frame, giving a constant filter but with the ability to vary amplitude and pitch. This gives a 10-bit frame. Finally, unvoiced frames are signaled by the pitch value's being zero. For these, only four reflection coefficients are transmitted, because the ear is relatively insensitive to spectral detail in unvoiced speech. This gives a 28-bit frame. The end of the utterance is signaled by the energy bits all being 1.

2.3. FORMANT SYNTHESIZERS: COMPUTALKER

The Computalker speech synthesizer appeared two years before the TI chip, in 1976. It was aimed primarily at the burgeoning computer hobbies market. One of its most far-reaching effects was to stimulate the interest of hobbyists, always eager for new low-cost peripherals, in speech synthesis. By doing this it has provided a useful new source of experimentation and expertise. Computalker is certainly the longest-lived and probably the most popular hobbyist's speech synthesizer.

It uses quite a different technique from the TI chip. Although we didn't go into the details of how linear predictive synthesis and the TI chip actually work, it is in fact a *digital* device. It contains digital adders and multipliers, just like a fullfledged computer. However, digital technology has only recently matured to the point where the operations needed to synthesize a speech waveform can be accomplished in real time, at reasonable cost. Until recently almost all speech synthesizers were analog devices—more like radio receivers than computers. They certainly do not use the linear prediction technique, for it cannot be implemented in analog hardware. Computalker, then, is an analog speech synthesizer, typical of the type that has actually been around in research laboratories for the past two decades. Of course, it uses present-day construction methods for analog hardware and so is much smaller and cheaper than the older synthesizers.

The principle on which it works, along with many other synthesizers, is to emulate the waveform produced in human speech by copying the pattern of formants. Recall from the last chapter that formants are resonances of the vocal tract, just like the resonances of an organ pipe, but they move around in frequency to give the vowel sounds their different characters. The source-filter model of speech says, in essence, that when you speak you generate a sound with your larynx, and the frequency characteristics of that sound are modified as it passes up through the vocal tract to emerge from your lips.

The source-filter model can be used as the basis for a speech synthesizer design. What we need to do is to simulate electronically the waveform produced by the larynx, and to simulate also the resonance effects of the vocal tract—in other words, the formants. A suitable waveform generator can easily be constructed to act as the source. We need to be able to control the frequency and amplitude of the waveform, for these correspond to the pitch and loudness of the voice. Electronic filters are needed, one to simulate each formant. The main thing to control here is their resonant frequency, for it will determine the vowel quality. More realistic speech sounds can be made if the bandwidth and amplification of the filters can be controlled as well, although these are very much second-order effects and cannot be varied in Computalker.

Of course, not all speech is voiced. The difference between fricative or hissy sounds and aspirated or whispered ones was outlined in the last chapter. Both can be produced by substituting a random noise generator for the sound source. In the case of aspiration, you make it with your larynx and it has to pass up through the vocal tract. On the way it is modified by the formant resonances. In other words, the source-filter configuration required is exactly the same as for voiced sounds, except that the sound source is different. Fricative noises, however, can be produced in conjunction with voiced sounds as in the voiced fricatives *z*, *zh*, *v*, and *dh*. For this reason an additional channel is needed for frication. To make the differences between the various fricatives, namely *s*, *sh*, *f*, and *th*, another filter is needed. The requirements for this are actually very similar to those of an ordinary formant filter. In fact, this extra filter is often called the *fricative formant filter*.

The Computalker is a straightforward implementation of the kind of synthesizer that we have sketched out. A block diagram of it is shown in Figure 2.11. In the center is the main vocal tract path, with three formant filters whose resonant frequencies can be controlled individually. The big arrows show the control parameters, and F1, F2, and F3 govern the frequencies of the three formants. A separate nasal branch in parallel with the oral one is provided, with a nasal formant of fixed frequency. This addition helps to produce realistic nasal sounds like *m*, *n*, and *ng*. It is less important to be able to vary the nasal formant frequency than it is for the oral ones, because the size and shape of the nasal tract is relatively fixed. However, you have to be able to control the nasal amplitude, in particular to turn it off during nonnasal sounds. Computalker provides an independent nasal amplitude parameter, marked as AN.

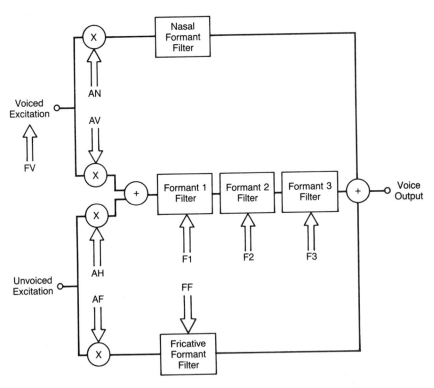

Figure 2.11 Block diagram of the Computalker.

Unvoiced excitation can be passed through the main vocal tract by using the aspiration amplitude control AH. In practice, the voicing amplitude AV will probably always be zero when AH is nonzero, for physiological constraints prohibit simultaneous voicing and aspiration. A second unvoiced excitation path passes through a fricative formant filter whose resonant frequency can be varied using the parameter FF. The amplitude of this is independently controlled by AF. Finally, the overall frequency of voicing—the pitch of the voice—is controlled by the FV parameter.

2.3.1. Controlling Computalker

Table 2.2 summarizes the nine parameters which drive Computalker. Four of them control amplitudes, while the others control frequencies. In the case of frequencies, the parameter value is logarithmically related to the actual frequency of the excitation or resonance. The ranges over which each frequency can be controlled is shown in the table.

TABLE 2.2 COMPUTALKER CONTROL PARAMETERS

name		meaning	width	range
0	AV	amplitude of voicing	8 bits	
1	AN	nasal amplitude	8 bits	
2	AH	amplitude of aspiration	8 bits	
3	AF	amplitude of frication	8 bits	
4	FV	fundamental frequency of voicing	8 bits	75 – 470 Hz
5	F1	formant 1 resonant frequency	8 bits	170 – 1450 Hz
6	F2	formant 2 resonant frequency	8 bits	520 – 4400 Hz
7	F3	formant 3 resonant frequency	8 bits	1700 – 5500 Hz
8	FF	fricative resonant frequency	8 bits	1700 – 14,000 Hz
9		not used		
10		not used		
11		not used		
12		not used		
13		not used		
14		not used		
15	SW	audio on-off switch	1 bit	

Each parameter is specified to Computalker as an 8-bit number. Every time your computer sends a parameter value to Computalker, it has to specify which parameter it is. This is done with a 4-bit code, so a total of twelve bits is transferred in parallel to Computalker from the computer for each parameter update. A complete set or *frame* of parameters is transferred by a sequence of nine of these 12-bit updates. Parameters 9 to 14 are unused ("reserved for future expansion" is the official phrase), and the last parameter, SW, governs the position of an audio on-off switch.

Since each of the nine parameters is sent regularly to Computalker, the controlling computer has to store or generate a set of nine graphs of parameter value against time. These graphs are usually called parameter *tracks*. This terminology is a hangover from the old days before computers, when parameter values for synthesizers were stored by painting them in conducting ink on glass slides. They picked up current off a coil of wire like the slider picks up current off a potentiometer. This generated a voltage which was controlled by the vertical position of the track. Nowadays the "tracks" are stored digitally, but the word is still used.

Unlike the TI chip, Computalker does not constrain the controlling computer to update the parameters at a fixed rate. The timing of updates is entirely up to the host computer. Typically, a 10 msec interval between frames is used. In fact the frame interval can be anywhere between 2 msec and 50 msec, and can be changed to alter the rate of speaking. However, it is rather naive to view fast speech as slow speech speeded up by a uniform time compression, for in human speech production the rhythm changes and elisions occur in a rather more subtle way. Thus it is not particularly useful to be able to alter the frame rate.

For each frame, the host computer transfers values for all of the nine parameters to Computalker, a total of 108 data bits. In theory, perhaps, it is necessary to transmit only those parameters whose values have changed, but in practice all of them should be updated regardless. This is because the parameters are stored for the duration of the frame in analog sample-and-hold devices. Essentially, the parameter value is represented as the charge on a capacitor. In time—and it takes only a short time—the values drift. Although the drift over 10 ms is insignificant, it becomes very noticeable over longer time periods. If parameters are not updated at all, the result is a "whooosh" sound up to maximum amplitude, in a period of a second or two. Hence it is essential that Computalker be serviced by the computer regularly, to update all its parameters. The audio on-off switch is provided so that the computer can turn off the sound directly if another program, which does not use the device, is to be run.

2.3.2. Market Orientation   As mentioned above, Computalker was designed for the computer hobbies market. Figure 2.12 shows a photograph of the device. It plugs into the S-100 bus which has been a *de facto* standard for hobbyists for several years and has recently been adopted as a standard by the Institute of Electrical and Electronic Engineers. This makes it immediately accessible to many microcomputer systems.

An inexpensive synthesis-by-rule program, of the kind to be described in the next chapter, is available to drive Computalker. It runs on the popular 8080 microprocessor. The input is coded in a machine-readable version of the standard phonetic alphabet, similar to that of Table 1.1. Stress digits may appear in the transcription, and the program caters for five levels of stress. The punctuation mark at the end of an utterance has some effect on pitch. The program is perhaps remarkable in that it occupies only 6 Kbyte of storage including

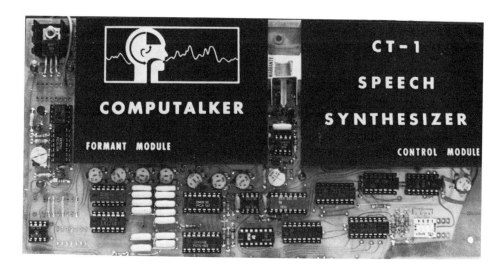

Figure 2.12 Computalker speech synthesizer.

phoneme tables, and runs on an 8-bit microprocessor. It is, however, *un*remarkable in that it produces very poor quality speech. According to a demonstration cassette, "Most people find the speech to be readily intelligible, especially after a little practice listening to it," but this is extremely optimistic. It also cunningly insinuates that if you don't understand it, you yourself may share the blame with the synthesizer—after all, *most* people do! Nevertheless, Computalker has made synthetic speech accessible to a large number of home computer users.

2.4. SOUND-SEGMENT SYNTHESIZERS: VOTRAX

Votrax was the first fully commercial speech synthesizer, and at the time of writing is still the only widely used speech output peripheral which works from a phonetic-style input instead of storing parameters extracted from natural utterances. Figure 2.13 shows a photograph of the Votrax model ML-I.

As far as the user is concerned, Votrax is quite different from the other two synthesizers we have discussed. It accepts as input a string of codes representing sound segments, each with additional bits to control the duration and pitch of the segment. In the earlier models there were 63 sound segments, specified by a 6-bit code, and two further bits accompanied each segment to provide a 4-level control over pitch. Four pitch levels are quite inadequate to generate acceptable intonation for anything but isolated words spoken in citation form. However, the ML-I uses an 8-level pitch specification, as well as a 4-level duration qualifier, associated with each sound segment. It provides a vocabulary of

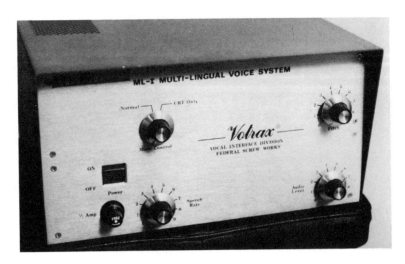

Figure 2.13 Votrax ML-I speech synthesizer.

80 sound segments. A further, low-cost model is available which plugs into the S-100 bus and is aimed primarily at computer hobbyists. The device has recently been packaged in a single chip using analog switched-capacitor filter technology.

One point where the ML-I scores favorably over other speech synthesis peripherals is the remarkably convenient engineering of its computer interface. It can be interposed between a display screen and the wire that connects it to the computer. The screen can be used quite normally, except that a special sequence of characters will cause Votrax to intercept the following message up to another special character and interpret it as speech. The operation is completely invisible, because the characters which specify the spoken message do not appear on the screen. However, there is a switch on the synthesizer which makes the characters appear so that you can check the sound-segment character sequence visually.

There is a problem with speech synthesizers because the computer can usually generate utterances much faster than the synthesizer can say them. To get around this, Votrax has its own store that can hold up to 64 sound segments. The computer can load this store as quickly as it wants, and then Votrax will empty it as the speech proceeds. Sixty-four segments are enough to generate small spoken messages. For longer passages, Votrax can be synchronized with the computer by using special control wires, together with an appropriate program to drive the device.

This is a particularly convenient interfacing technique. As an example of how it can be used, you can arrange computer files, each of whose lines contain a printed message, together with its Votrax equivalent bracketed by the appropriate control characters. When the file is listed or examined with an editor program, the lines appear simultaneously in spoken and typed English.

The internal workings of Votrax are not divulged by the manufacturer. Figure 2.14 shows a block diagram at the level of detail that they supply. It seems to be essentially a formant synthesizer, like Computalker. However, analog function generators and parameter smoothing circuits provide transitions between sound segments.

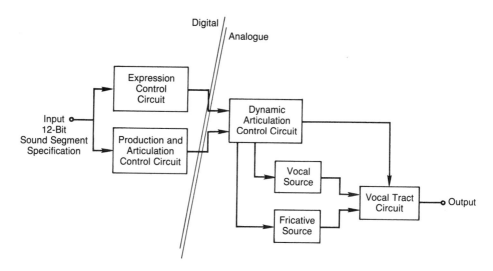

Figure 2.14 Block diagram of Votrax.

2.4.1. Sound Segments

The 80 segments of the high-range ML-I model are summarized in Table 2.3. They are divided into phoneme classes. Somewhat under half of the segments correspond directly with English phonemes. Many of the others are variants of the vowels with the same sound quality but different durations. The rest are either allophonic variations or additional sounds which can sensibly be combined with certain phonemes in certain contexts. For example, AY is an allophone of I; it sounds slightly different. But .PH is not an allophone, but a sound burst which can be used in conjunction with P to make it more prominent. The Votrax literature and consequently Votrax users persist in calling all elements "phonemes," and this can cause considerable confusion. I prefer to use the term *sound segment* instead, reserving "phoneme" for its proper linguistic use.

The rules which Votrax uses for transitions between sound segments are not made public by the manufacturer and are embedded in encapsulated circuits in the hardware. They are clearly very crude. The key to successful encoding of utterances is to use the many nonphonemic segments in an appropriate way

TABLE 2.3   VOTRAX SOUND SEGMENTS AND THEIR DURATIONS

	Votrax		duration (msec)	example word
i	I		118	hid
	I1	(sound equivalent of I)	83	
	I2	(sound equivalent of I)	58	
	I3	(allophone of I)	58	
	.I3	(sound equivalent of I3)	83	
	AY	(allophone of I)	65	
e	EH		118	head
	EH1	(sound equivalent of EH)	70	
	EH2	(sound equivalent of EH)	60	
	EH3	(allophone of EH)	60	
	.EH2	(sound equivalent of EH3)	70	
	A1	(allophone of EH)	100	
	A2	(sound equivalent of A1)	95	
aa	AE		100	had
	AE1	(sound equivalent of AE)	100	
o	AW		235	hod
	AW2	(sound equivalent of AW)	90	
	AW1	(allophone of AW)	143	
u	OO		178	hood
	OO1	(sound equivalent of OO)	103	
	IU	(allophone of OO)	63	
a	UH		103	hud
	UH1	(sound equivalent of UH)	95	
	UH2	(sound equivalent of UH)	50	
	UH3	(allophone of UH)	70	
	.UH3	(sound equivalent of UH3)	103	
	.UH2	(allophone of UH)	60	
ar	AH1		143	hard
	AH2	(sound equivalent of AH1)	70	
aw	O		178	hawed
	O1	(sound equivalent of O)	118	
	O2	(sound equivalent of O)	83	
	.O	(allophone of O)	178	
	.O1	(sound equivalent of .O)	123	
	.O2	(sound equivalent of .O)	90	
uu	U		178	who'd
	U1	(sound equivalent of U)	90	
er	ER		143	heard
ee	E		178	heed
	E1	(sound equivalent of E)	118	
r	R		90	
	.R	(allophone of R)	50	
w	W		83	
	.W	(allophone of W)	83	

TABLE 2.3 VOTRAX SOUND SEGMENTS AND THEIR DURATIONS (CONTINUED)

	Votrax		duration (msec)	example word
l	L		105	
	L1	(allophone of L)	105	
y	Y		103	
	Y1	(allophone of Y)	83	
m	M		105	
b	B		70	
p	P		100	
	.PH	(aspiration burst for use with P)	88	
n	N		83	
d	D		50	
	.D	(allophone of D)	53	
t	T		90	
	DT	(allophone of T)	50	
	.S	(aspiration burst for use with T)	70	
ng	NG		120	
g	G		75	
	.G	(allophone of G)	75	
k	K		75	
	.K	(allophone of K)	80	
	.X1	(aspiration burst for use with K)	68	
s	S		90	
z	Z		70	
sh	SH		118	
	CH	(allophone of SH)	55	
zh	ZH		90	
	J	(allophone of ZH)	50	
f	F		100	
v	V		70	
th	TH		70	
dh	THV		70	
h	H		70	
	H1	(allophone of H)	70	
	.H1	(allophone of H)	48	
silence	PA0		45	
	PA1		175	
	.PA1		5	
	.PA2	(used to change amplitude and duration)	0	

as transitions between the main segments which represent phonetic classes. This is a tricky process, and I have heard of people giving up in despair at the extreme difficulty of generating the utterances they want. Nevertheless, with luck, skill, and especially persistence, excellent results can be obtained. The

ML-I manual contains a list of about 625 words and short phrases, and most of them are clearly recognizable.

2.4.2. Duration and Pitch Qualifiers

Each sound segment has a different duration. Table 2.3 shows the measured duration of the segments, although no calibration data is given by Votrax. As mentioned earlier, a 2-bit number accompanies each segment to modify its duration. This allows a segment to be uttered with three additional durations, longer than those in the table.

As well as the rate qualifier, each sound segment is accompanied by a 3-bit pitch specification. This provides control over the fundamental frequency. The quantization interval varies from one to two semitones. Votrax interpolates pitch from phoneme to phoneme in a highly satisfactory manner, and this permits surprisingly sophisticated intonation patterns to be generated considering the crude 8-level quantization.

2.5. DISCUSSION

We have looked at four different kinds of device for generating the speech waveform. The first was direct recording of the raw waveform. Although analog techniques have traditionally been used for this, the requirement of rapid access to prerecorded messages makes digital technology much more suitable for the purpose of making computers talk. The method is very simple. Samples of the speech waveform are taken and stored during the recording process and regenerated upon replay. You need to sample quite often—at least 8000 times per second—and each sample needs seven to twelve bits for storage, depending on whether logarithmic or linear quantization is used. This implies a substantial data rate, so that a large amount of storage might be needed.

However, the cost of storage is not the only drawback to direct recording. Although the quality of reproduction will be fairly good, the method is inflexible in that utterances must be recorded and stored in their entirety to sound completely natural. Mix-and-match selection of words or phrases is difficult, because when they are put together out of context the intonation sounds wrong.

The Speak 'n Spell toy uses the method of linear prediction, as in fact do many other present-day systems. Linear prediction is a way of extracting parameters from a speech waveform which describe the vocal tract configuration of the speaker. There are twelve parameters, one each for pitch and amplitude, and ten to represent the vocal tract shape. Because physiology prohibits rapid changes in the positions of vocal organs, the parameters need to be sampled and stored only fifty times a second. Further coding techniques reduce the average data rate to 1.2 Kbit/s, so that quite a lot of speech can be put into the two read-only memory chips in the Speak 'n Spell toy. To regenerate speech from the stored data, a special chip is used to implement the algorithm for linear predictive synthesis.

Linear prediction has another advantage over direct recording, apart from a fifty-fold reduction in data storage requirements. Because it separates pitch and amplitude from the other parameters, it is quite feasible to regenerate the speech with a different pitch pattern—in other words, with a different intonation. This makes it possible to mix and match separately recorded words and phrases, and apply an overall intonation to the result to try and make a homogeneous, natural-sounding, utterance. We will return to this in Chapter 4.

The next method, formant synthesis, is used in the Computalker speech peripheral, and in other devices. Older than linear prediction, it uses the same basic idea of describing the waveform with slowly varying parameters. The sampling rate and number of parameters are comparable with linear prediction. Pitch and amplitude are again two of the parameters, but the others are related to the frequencies of the formant resonances rather than to the vocal tract shape. From the point of view of the user, the chief difference between the methods is that it is easier to extract linear predictive parameters directly from a live utterance, but for formant synthesizers there is more readily available published data about the positions of formant resonances in vowels and other phonemes of speech. You find that formant synthesizers are popular in systems for generating speech from phonetics or text, while linear predictive ones are more common in systems which store and replay human utterances. Another difference is that linear predictive devices have to be implemented digitally, whereas formant synthesizers like Computalker can be all analog.

The fourth device, Votrax, is actually an analog formant synthesizer like Computalker. But it looks quite different to the user, for it contains on-board circuitry for emulating speech sounds. It is not driven by parameters, but has a vocabulary of sound segments which can be called up as required. It would be nice if these sound segments were actually phonemes, but they form a lower-level representation because transitions are not taken account of properly. Although Votrax is rather difficult to use, it requires a much lower data rate than the other methods and is capable of generating quite good speech. However, its on-board sound generation takes control away from the user, and you find that people interested in high-quality speech, or in research on speech generation methods, rarely use Votrax but opt for one of the lower-level devices. Also, it is quite impossible to take a human utterance and analyze it into Votrax sound segments so that it can be resynthesized.

2.6. FURTHER READING

Flanagan, J.L., *Speech Analysis, Synthesis, and Perception*. Berlin: Springer Verlag, 1972. This book is the speech researcher's bible, and like the Bible, it's not all that easy to read. However, it is an essential reference source for speech acoustics and speech synthesis (as well as for human speech perception).

Flanagan, J.L. and L.R. Rabiner, eds., *Speech Synthesis*. Stroudsburg, Pennsylvania: Dowden, Hutchinson, and Ross, 1973. This is a collection of previously published research papers on speech synthesis, rather than a unified book. It contains most of the classic papers on the subject from 1940 to 1972 and is a very useful reference work.

Garrett, P.H., *Analog Systems for Microprocessors and Minicomputers*. Reston, Virginia: Reston Publishing Company, 1978. Garrett discusses the technology of data conversion hardware, including A/D and D/A converters and basic analog filter design, in a clear and practical manner.

Holmes, J.N., *Speech Synthesis*. London, England: Mills and Boom, 1972. This little book, by one of Britain's foremost workers in the field, introduces the subject of speech synthesis and speech synthesizers.

Rabiner, L.R. and R.W. Schafer, *Digital Processing of Speech Signals*. Englewood Cliffs, New Jersey: Prentice-Hall Inc., 1978. This is probably the best single reference for digital speech analysis. If you want to find out about ways of compressing the speech waveform, or to go deeper into the theory of sampling and quantization, try it. Be warned in advance, however, that it takes a fairly theoretical approach to the subject.

3

The Segment Level:
Joining Pieces Together

The obvious way to make computers talk is to choose some basic acoustic units to be used, record them, and construct new utterances by the mix-and-match method, joining together appropriate pieces from this dictionary. The crucial question then becomes, what are the basic units? Should they be whole sentences, words, syllables, or phonemes?

When selecting the basic units, you have to consider several factors. The larger they are, the more utterances have to be stored in the dictionary. English has 26 letters, thousands of syllables, tens of thousands of words, millions of short phrases, and a limitless number of sentences. This growth is depicted in Figure 3.1. It is not so much the length of each individual utterance that matters, but rather the number of different ones needed. This tends to increase very quickly as the size of the basic unit increases.

Numbers provide an excellent example. There are only ten digits, but ten million 7-digit telephone numbers. You certainly don't want to have to record each one individually. The problem is partly one of providing enough storage for the dictionary of utterances. But as storage technology improves, the limitation is becoming more and more one of recording the utterances in the first place. A 300-Mbyte disk can hold around ten hours of speech digitized at 64 Kbit/s. With linear predictive coding, as used in the Speak 'n Spell toy, it can hold nearly a month of speech. And this is a month of 7-day weeks with 24 hours each day, and continuous speech—without pauses. Setting up a recording session to fill the disk would certainly be a big job.

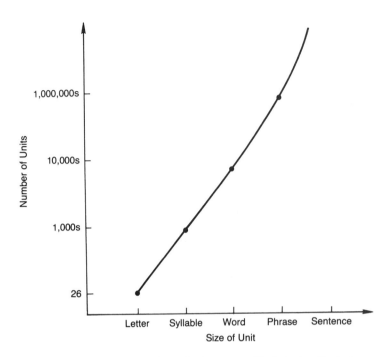

Figure 3.1 How the number of units grows with their size, for text.

In written language, we use the word as a basic unit. Sentences are built from words, and it is words rather than sentences that are kept in things like dictionaries and spelling lists. The word seems to be a sensibly sized basic unit for speech, too. Many applications of talking computers use a rather limited vocabulary of words. A large dictionary of 50,000 words, each lasting between half a second and a second, could be kept on the 300-Mbyte disk, even using direct digitized recording at 64 Kbit/s. Unfortunately, with this technique we get problems when we try to join words together.

Real speech is connected. There are few gaps between words. If you find this hard to believe, listen to someone speaking in a foreign language that you don't understand at all. Can you tell the words apart? And sounds in speech are very strongly affected by those on either side of them. You just have to think of the way your tongue and jaws move when you are speaking to convince yourself of this. Naturally, these effects operate across word boundaries. Since the time duration of their influences is governed by the mechanics of the vocal tract, periods of tens or hundreds of milliseconds are involved. Now the pitch period of a normal male speaking voice at 100 Hz is only 10 ms. Thus the effects straddle several pitch periods and cannot be simulated by simply smoothing the speech waveforms together.

Features of intonation span much longer stretches of speech than single words, like phrases or whole sentences. For many applications of computer speech, intonation is most important at the utterance level of a single, sentence-sized, information unit. If speech waveforms of individual words are stored, utterances cannot be given a homogeneous intonation. It is not feasible to alter the fundamental frequency or duration of a time waveform without changing all the formant resonances as well.

However, if the speech is stored in either linear predictive form or as parameters for a formant synthesizer, both word-to-word influences and the essential features of intonation can be incorporated. In terms of the source-filter model of speech production, which we encountered in the first chapter, this is because the influence of the sound source has been separated from that of the filter. We look in the next section at joining words stored in this form, while the problems of intonation are left to the next chapter.

For more general applications of speech output, there are limitations to word storage which soon become apparent. Although most people's daily vocabularies are surprisingly small, most words have a number of inflected forms. For example, the base word "word" gives rise to "words," "wordy," "wording," "wordings, "worded," "wordiness"; not to mention "word-painting," "word-perfect," "word-picture," "word-play," "word-splitting," and so on. These need to be recorded and stored separately if we adopt a strict policy of word storage. For instance, in this book there are about 54,000 words, and 6000 (11 percent) different ones, counting inflected forms. In Chapter 1 alone, there are 8000 words and 2000 (25 percent) different ones.

It seems crazy to treat a simple inflection like -s as a completely different word from the base form. But once you consider storing roots and endings separately, you begin to find that there are vast numbers of different endings, and it is difficult to know where to draw the line. It is natural to think instead of simply using the syllable as the basic unit.

A reasonable estimate of the number of different syllables in English is ten thousand. (Actually, it all depends on what you mean by "syllable"—it is a surprisingly difficult thing to define.) At three a second, only about an hour's storage is required for them all. But waveform storage will certainly not do. Although the effects of one word on another need to be taken into account to make speech sound fluent, effects of one syllable on another need to be imitated for it even to be *intelligible*. Adopting a source-filter kind of representation like linear prediction or formant parameters is essential. You need some scheme for smoothing the parameters between syllables which simulates the movement of the vocal tract from one posture to another. Unfortunately, a great deal of action occurs in the speech waveform at syllable boundaries. Stops are exploded, the sound source changes between voicing and frication, and so on. Perhaps we should store instead "inverse syllables," comprising a vowel-consonant-vowel sequence instead of consonant-vowel-consonant. For example, the syllables in "making computers talk" are "m a k | k i n g | c o m | p u t | t e r s | t a l k"

(using English letters rather than phonemes). Inverse syllables are

"m a | a k i | i n g c o | o m p u | u t e | e r s t a | a l k"

These have jokingly been dubbed "lisibles." Since most of the difficult acoustic changes occur on consonants rather than in the middle of vowels, it is probably easier to join vowel-consonant-vowel units together.

Again, you will encounter big practical problems if you try to create an inventory of syllables, or of lisibles. Now it is not so much the recording that is hard, but the editing needed to ensure that the cuts between syllables are made at exactly the right point. As units get smaller, the exact placement of the boundaries becomes even more critical. Several thousand sensitive sound-editing jobs should not be undertaken lightly.

We have mentioned joining together syllables and inverse syllables. If you are able to join speech satisfactorily at syllable boundaries and in the middle of syllables, you might consider using smaller, half-syllable units. Then the example becomes

"m a | a k | k i | i n g | c o | o m | p u | u t | t e | e r s | t a | a l k"

This reduces the size of the segment inventory to an estimated one to two thousand entries, and the tedious job of editing each one individually becomes at least feasible, if not enviable. As an alternative to recording a human voice, the segment dictionary could be created by artificial means involving cut-and-try experiments with the parameters of the synthesizer.

The ultimate in economy of dictionary size, of course, is to use phonemes as the basic unit, giving for the example

"m e i k i ng k uh m p y uu t er z t aw k"

This makes the most critical part of the job joining the units together, rather than constructing or recording them. With only about forty phonemes in English, each one can be examined in many different contexts to ascertain the best information to store. There is no need to record them directly from a human voice—it would be difficult anyway, for many phonemes cannot be produced in isolation. In fact, a phoneme is an abstract unit, not a particular sound, so it is best to generate data by looking at several different instances rather than making an exact record of just one.

We saw in the first chapter that a given phoneme sounds different in different contexts. The various sounds that a phoneme may have are called *allophones* of the phoneme. There are several allophones corresponding to each phoneme. If you store data about phonemes, allophones have to be created by altering the transitions between units, and to a lesser extent by modifying the central parts of the units themselves. The rules for making transitions will have a big effect on the quality of the resulting speech.

Instead of trying to perform this task automatically by a computer program, the allophones themselves could be stored. This will make it somewhat easier to generate transitions between segments, although the job will certainly not be trivial. The total number of allophones will depend on the narrowness of the transcription system. Sixty to eighty is typical, and it is unlikely to exceed one or two hundred. In any case there will not be a storage problem. However, now when you code an utterance for the computer to speak, you have to produce an allophonic transcription. If you are skillful and patient, you should be able to coax the system into producing fairly understandable speech, but the effort required for this on a per-utterance basis should not be underestimated. This is the approach taken by the Votrax synthesizer discussed in the previous chapter.

TABLE 3.1   FACTORS IN CHOOSING THE BASIC UNIT

	Size of utterance inventory	Storage method	Source of utterance inventory	Principal burden is placed on
sentences	depends on application	waveform or source-filter parameters	natural speech	recording artist, storage medium
words	depends on application	source-filter parameters	natural speech	recording artist and editor, storage medium
syllables/lisibles	10,000	source-filter parameters	natural speech	recording editor
half-syllables	1,000	source-filter parameters	natural speech or artificially generated	recording editor or inventory compiler
phonemes	40	generalized parameters	artificially generated	author of segment concatenation program
allophones	50—100	generalized or source-filter parameters	artificially generated or natural speech	coder of synthesized utterances

Table 3.1 summarizes in broad brush strokes the issues which affect the choice of basic unit for joining together, and Figure 3.2 shows how the number of individual units changes as the size of each one grows. In the sections which follow, we will look in more detail at the different methods. We will leave the important problems of prosody to the next chapter and consider only the segmental aspects here. All of the methods rely to some extent on the acoustic

properties of speech, and as smaller basic units are considered the role of speech acoustics becomes more important. It is impossible in a book like this to give a detailed account of acoustic phonetics, for it would take several volumes. What we do in the following pages is to examine some important features which are relevant to joining pieces of speech together.

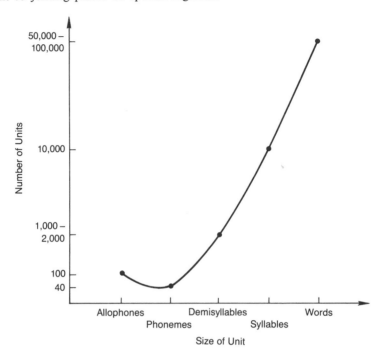

Figure 3.2 How the number of units grows with their size, for speech.

3.1. JOINING WORDS

Using words as the basic unit is an inherently limited technique because of the large number of them. For the present purpose, when I say "words" I mean phonetically different words—words which sound different. For example, to *wind* and the *wind* are phonetically different, in spite of the fact that they are written the same. On the other hand, *piece* and *peace* are phonetically identical. But the real problem stems from the great variety of word endings—recall the "word," "words," "wordy" example above—and the fact that different endings make phonetically different words. Despite its inherent limitations, this is at present the most widely used synthesis method, and is likely to remain so for several years. We have seen that the primary problems are the sound differences introduced by the influence of one word on its neighbor and prosody.

Both can be overcome, at least to a useful approximation, by coding the words in source-filter form, either as linear prediction parameters or formant parameters.

3.1.1. Words Stored as Waveforms   Nevertheless, a surprising number of applications simply store the time waveform. It is unusual to store the digitized waveform directly at 64 Kbit/s (or a similar rate), because there are quite simple techniques which can be used to reduce the data to a half or a third of this. We will not be concerned with data reduction for speech waveforms, for it is a technical matter which is not of particular interest. The point is that even if data reduction is used, it is effectively the raw waveform that is stored.

For the designer of a computer speech system, waveform storage has many advantages. Speech quality can easily be controlled by selecting a suitable sampling rate and coding scheme. A natural-sounding voice is guaranteed; male or female as desired. The equipment required is minimal—a digital-to-analog converter and some filtering hardware will do for synthesis if direct digitization is used. The hardware required for more efficient coding methods is not much more complicated.

It is impossible to make completely fluent utterances by joining together the waveforms of individually recorded words. We discussed this in the last chapter. If the words are recorded on an analog medium like a tape recorder, a major problem is the introduction of clicks and other interference between words. It it is difficult to prevent discontinuities between the end of the time waveform of one word and the start of that of the next, as shown in Figure 3.3(a). These discontinuities will cause clicks which are surprisingly distracting.

Boundary discontinuities present no problem with digital storage, however, for the waveforms can be edited accurately before they are stored so that they start and finish at an exactly zero level [Figure 3.3(b)]. With digital techniques, the lack of fluency stems from the absence of proper control of context effects between words, and, of course, prosody.

This is not necessarily a serious drawback if the application is a sufficiently limited one. Complete utterances which never change can be stored as one unit, and will sound excellent. Often sentences can be viewed as templates with slots which can be filled in by a number of different words, as in

There are ... messages for you

and

Invoice number ..., for a shipment of ... to ..., is outstanding

Then, each slot-filling word is recorded in an intonation consistent both with its position in the template utterance and with the intonation of that utterance. This could be done by embedding the word in the utterance for recording, and

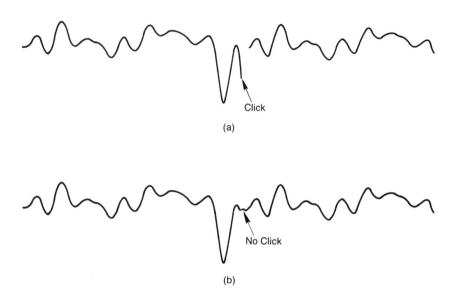

Figure 3.3 (a) Click introduced by a discontinuity when joining waveforms (b) Waveforms
adjusted to avoid the click.

extracting it by digital editing before storage. It would be difficult to try to
take into account the effects of context on the sounds, however, for this would
mean that the template must be made consistent with several different slot-
fillers. The problem could perhaps be alleviated if several versions of the template were stored, but then the number of versions required would become very
large if there were more than one slot in a single utterance. But it is not really
necessary, for the lack of fluency will probably be interpreted by a benevolent
listener as an attempt to convey the information as clearly as possible. Because
a fluent transition cannot be obtained, it is best to leave slight gaps on each side
of the slot-filling word.

Difficulties will occur if the same slot-filler is used in different contexts.
For instance, the first gap in each of the sentences above contains a number; yet
the intonation of the number may need to be different in each case. Many systems simply ignore this problem and use the same version of the number in each
context. Then when you hear the speech you will probably notice anomalies,
especially if you listen for them. The words come, as it were, from different
mouths, without fluency. But in practice, this often doesn't matter too much.
If it is found to be distracting, two or more versions of each slot-filler can be
recorded, one for each context.

As an example, suppose you plan to join together digits to form seven-
digit telephone numbers like 289−5371. If you store only one version of each
digit, record it in a level tone of voice. Also, insert a pause after the third

digit, for this is how people say telephone numbers. The resulting synthetic speech will certainly be unnatural, although it should be clear and intelligible. If by any chance one of the digits was recorded on a rising or falling intonation, rather than a level one, numbers containing it will sound peculiar.

At the other extreme, you might consider recording and storing one version of each digit for each position in the number. Since there are seven possible positions, you would need seven recordings of "0," seven of "1," and so on—70 single-digit recordings in all. The recording would be extremely tedious. Mistakes in intonation would certainly be made during recording, and several recording sessions would be needed. Even if all errors were ironed out, the synthetic utterances would still not be fluent, because phonetic context effects between one word and the next are not taken into account. Instead, they would sound as though the speaker was trying to enunciate his speech unnaturally clearly.

A good compromise is to record only three versions of each digit. One is for any of the five positions xx −xxx . The next is for the third position   x −   . The last is for the final position   −   x. The first version should be in a level voice; the second an incomplete, rising tone; and the third a final, dropping pitch.

3.1.2. Words Stored as Parameters

There are two separate limitations to the time-domain method. The first is the lack of fluency caused by unnatural transitions between words. The second is the large number of utterances that will have to be stored if you decide to record the same word several times in different contexts. Even if you opt for a compromise solution like the one above, you will probably have to do a lot of experimentation before you are sure that a good balance has been struck between the sound quality and the recording and storage costs. These problems can be alleviated by storing a parametric representation instead of the waveform. As we saw in the last chapter, the parameters could either be formant-based ones, or linear predictive ones.

When utterances are stored parametrically, it is possible to run them together more smoothly. Also, since the pitch has now been isolated from the rest of the speech as a separate parameter, you can apply a new, complete pitch pattern to the utterance as a whole. Thus you can synthesize a sequence of words with a natural overall intonation, even though they were not recorded together originally. Even then, you still cannot expect to hear conversational speech. This is because rhythmical effects in natural speech tend to stretch some words and shrink others in a complicated way, and this cannot really be taken into account properly without descending below the word level.

Should you use formant parameters or linear predictive ones? As far as joining the words together is concerned, it doesn't really matter—the techniques are essentially the same for both, and you will get similar results. The choice really depends on which makes it easier for the *recording* end of the process.

It is not particularly easy to record an utterance and obtain formant tracks for it. There are ways of analyzing speech by computer algorithms and extracting the formant positions at each point in time. These methods are fairly complicated, but the real difficulty is that they are not particularly accurate. In practice, people generally have their computer perform such an analysis, and then inspect the formant tracks themselves. Knowing what was said, and with considerable skill and experience, one can spot where the problems occur and correct the tracks by hand. In this way you can get accurate values for the formant positions, and you can probably make the speech sound quite reasonable when replayed through a formant synthesizer like Computalker. People have in fact done this for short utterances to the point where the synthetic version is so like the original, natural one that you simply can't tell them apart—even under high-quality listening conditions with headphones. For such good synthetic speech, a considerably more sophisticated synthesizer than Computalker is needed, although the basic principles of operation are the same. However, to produce speech like this for a two-second utterance can take *several months* of a skilled person's time. So although it can give excellent results, hand-editing of formant parameters adds a whole new dimension to the problem of constructing a vocabulary. It is an exceedingly tiresome and time-consuming task.

The recording and analysis process is easier with the linear prediction method. Linear predictive analysis is usually done completely automatically, without any tweaking of parameters by hand. It does take a fairly complicated computer program, though, and requires a lot of number-crunching, so your computer will not be able to do it in real time unless it has specially fast arithmetic hardware. Actually, once you have got the linear prediction parameters, it is not hard to calculate the formant frequencies from them. But there is no need to do this, because the linear prediction parameters are quite suitable for direct use in the joining-up procedure.

Once you have decided what kind of parametric representation to use, and have recorded the utterances and encoded them satisfactorily, the process of joining words together does not present any great difficulty. There is not enough information in the parametrically encoded words to permit sophisticated techniques which take into account the phonetic influence of one word on the next. For a start, if either the end of the first or the beginning of the second word (or both) is a fricative, unnatural formant transitions do not matter, for they will probably not be noticed anyway. Smooth transitions from one fricative to another are rare in natural speech. Recall that the formants play a part only in voiced or aspirated speech. Even aspiration is probably not worth bothering about, because *h* is the only fully aspirated sound in English, and it is relatively uncommon.

Therefore, unless both sides of the junction are voiced, it is probably enough to abut the stored parameter tracks for the two words. It is important to realize that this is certainly *not* the same as simply abutting the time waveforms. In the case of parametric storage, a new set of parameters will be stored every 10 or 20 ms. Hence the transition will automatically be smoothed over this time period by the speech synthesizer hardware. This is quite different from directly joining the time waveforms, for here the transition takes place over a single sampling period. If we are sampling at a rate of 8 kHz, the transition will therefore be over in as little as 125 μsec, and so is a hundred times faster than when the parametric method is used.

For voiced-to-voiced transitions, more care should be taken to make a smooth join. To do this you first decide upon how long the transition should be. A typical value is 50 ms. The sets of parameter tracks for the two words on either side of the boundary will be overlapped for this amount of time. Next, the resonance parameters in the final 50 ms of the first word are averaged with those in the first 50 ms of the second. The average is weighted, with the first word's formants dominating at the beginning and their effect progressively dying out in favor of the second word.

More sophisticated than a simple average is to weight the components according to how rapidly they are changing. If the formant pattern in one word is changing much more quickly than that in the other, you might expect that this will dominate the transition. The overall rate of change of the parameters can be estimated quite easily. The estimate can then be used to load the averages during the transition in favor of the dominant side of the junction.

To make the joined words sound natural, it is much more important to look at the rhythm and intonation of the speech, rather than these picky details of exactly how the parameter tracks are merged with each other. We will do this in the next chapter.

A word-joining scheme like this has been implemented and tested on—guess what!—seven-digit telephone numbers! Significant improvement in people's ability to recall numbers was found for this method over direct abuttal of either natural or synthetic versions of the digits. Although the method seemed, on balance, to produce utterances that were recalled less accurately than completely natural spoken telephone numbers, the difference was not significant. The system was also used to generate wiring instructions by computer directly from the connection list; we will describe it in more detail in Chapter 5. The synthetic speech was actually preferred to natural speech in the noisy environment of the production line.

Some other considerations can be taken into account when joining words together, to improve the naturalness of the speech. For example, when you say a phrase like "stop burst," the plosion on the *p* of "stop" is normally suppressed because it is followed by another stop. This is a particularly striking case, because the place of articulation of the two stops *p* and *b* is the same. Complete suppression is not as likely to happen in "stop gap," for example, although it may occur. Here is an instance of how extra information could improve the quality of the synthetic transitions considerably. It would probably be best to mark the positions of stops, and their place of articulation, by hand when the words are recorded. To attempt it automatically would be a very difficult job.

Another possibility for improvement is to try to make the transition between two vowels sound more natural. By using the simple overlap-and-average method above, if one word ends with a vowel and the next begins with one, the two will tend to blur together. This is especially noticeable when the second word begins with a stressed syllable. Clearer, although often less natural, articulation can be achieved by placing a *glottal stop* at the juncture. The glottal stop is a sound used in many dialects of English. It frequently occurs in the utterance "uh-uh," meaning "no." Here it *is* used to separate two vowel sounds, but in fact this is not particularly common in most dialects. You could say "the apple," "the orange," "the onion" with a neutral vowel in "the" to rhyme with "*a*bove" and a glottal stop as separator, but it is much more usual to rhyme "the" with "he" and introduce a *y* between the words. Similarly, even if you don't normally pronounce an *r* at the end of words—some people do and some don't—you will probably use one in "bigger apple," rather than introducing a glottal stop. Note that it would be wrong to put an *r* in "the apple," even if you usually end "the" and "bigger" with the same sound. Such effects occur at a high level of processing, and are practically impossible to simulate within a word-joining system which operates on stored parameters. Hence it is probably a good idea to introduce a glottal stop between vowels, as suggested above, even though it is certainly unnatural.

3.2. JOINING SYLLABLES

The use of segments larger than a single phoneme but smaller than a word as the basic unit for speech synthesis has an interesting history. People have realized for a long time that transitions between phonemes are extremely sensitive and critical components of speech, so that it is essential to get them right for successful synthesis. Consider the unvoiced stop sounds p, t, and k. Their central portion is actually silent, as you will discover if you try saying a word like "butter" with a very long t. If you think about it, this means that it can *only* be the transitional information which distinguishes these sounds from one another.

Sound segments which span the transition from the center of one phoneme to the center of the next are called *dyads* or *diphones*. The possibility of synthesizing speech by joining them together was first mooted in the mid-1950s. The idea is attractive because a spectrogram shows relatively little change within the central, so-called "steady-state" portion of many phonemes. In the extreme case of unvoiced stops, for example, there is not only no movement but no spectrum at all in the steady state. At that time the formant synthesizer was in its infancy, and so recorded segments of live speech had to be used. The early experiments met with little success because of the technical difficulties of joining analog waveforms without clicks, and inevitable discrepancies between the steady-state parts of a phoneme recorded in different contexts.

In the mid-1960s, with the growing use of formant synthesizers, it became possible to generate diphones by copying formant frequencies manually from a spectrogram, and improving the result by trial and error. It was not feasible to extract formant frequencies automatically from real speech, though, because computers were slow and expensive, and the necessary techniques were only just being invented. For example, a project at IBM stored manually derived parameter tracks for diphones, identified by pairs of phoneme names. To make it say something, you typed in the utterance as phonemes, and the diphone table was used to give a set of parameter tracks. Since the inventory was synthetic, there was no difficulty in ensuring that discontinuities did not arise between segments beginning and ending with the same phoneme. This means that there is no problem in smoothing across boundaries. The resulting speech was reported to be quite impressive.

A diphone is a pair of phonemes. This is not quite the same thing as a half-syllable, properly called a *demisyllable*. In the simplest case they happen to be identical, for a consonant-vowel-consonant syllable is made from exactly two diphones. However, many syllables (like "splat" and "pants") begin or end with complicated consonant clusters which are not easy to produce convincingly by joining diphones. This means that there is an advantage to using demisyllables rather than diphones as the basic unit. But there are too many demisyllables for it to be easy to produce a complete dictionary of them by hand-editing resonance parameters, as was done for diphones in the project mentioned above. Fortunately, there is a way out. Since the mid-1960s, speech analysis methods have been developed and refined considerably. It is now possible to extract formant or linear prediction parameters automatically from natural utterances. For this reason, there has been a resurgence of interest in demisyllable and syllable synthesis methods. The wheel has turned full circle, from segments of natural speech to hand-tailored parameters and back again.

I said earlier that, from the point of view of storage capacity, there is an advantage to storing demisyllables over syllables. There are perhaps one to two thousand demisyllables in English, as opposed to four to ten thousand syllables. But this is probably not too significant with the continuing decline of storage costs. The requirements are of the order of 25 Kbyte versus 500 Kbyte for 1.2 Kbit/s linear predictive coding. Even the larger figure could almost be accommodated today on a state-of-the-art read-only memory chip.

A bigger advantage for demisyllables comes from considering the speech rhythm. As we will see in the next chapter, the rhythms of fluent speech cause dramatic variations in syllable duration. These variations seem to affect the vowel of the syllable and the cluster of consonants which follow the vowel, much more than the initial cluster of consonants. If you consider the beginning of a demisyllable to be shortly after the beginning of the vowel, when the formant structure has settled down, most of the vowel and the cluster of consonants which follow it will lie in a single demisyllable. The cluster of consonants at the beginning of the next syllable will lie in the next demisyllable. This makes it easier to lengthen just those parts that are stretched out in natural speech. If you use whole syllables, it is much more difficult to do this.

One system for joining demisyllables has produced excellent results for simple, monosyllabic English words. The demisyllable inventory is kept as small as possible by using syllable affixes s, z, t, and d, which are attached to the core of the syllable in a separate operation. Prosodic rather than segmental considerations are likely to prove the major limiting factor when this scheme is extended to running speech.

Here is how the system works. Monosyllabic words, spoken in isolation, are analyzed automatically into linear prediction coefficients. A person then segments the speech, by editing the parameter tracks on a computer, into the initial consonant cluster and the vowel plus final cluster. The cut is made partway (60 ms) into the vowel. This makes it easier to smooth the pieces together when segments are joined, for there is ample voicing on either side of the juncture. The parameters should not differ radically at the boundary, because the vowel is the same in each demisyllable. The junction is smoothed over a small (40 ms) overlap period.

An alternative smoothing rule applies when the second segment has a nasal or glide after the vowel. When this happens in live speech, the vowel sound is colored in anticipation of the nasal or glide, and this affects even the early part of the vowel. For example, a vowel is frequently nasalized when followed by a nasal sound. Under these circumstances the overlap area is moved forward in time so that the coloration applies throughout almost the whole vowel.

3.3. JOINING PHONEMES

Before we can discuss the problem of joining phonemes together, we will have to find out something about acoustic phonetics. Acoustic phonetics is the study of how the acoustic signal relates to the phonetic sequence which was spoken or heard. People—especially engineers—often ask, how could phonetics not be acoustic? In fact it can be articulatory, auditory, or linguistic, depending on whether you approach it from the point of view of how people speak, how they hear, or how they think. The invention of the sound spectrograph in the late 1940s was hailed as an event of colossal significance for acoustic phonetics, for it somehow seemed to make the intricacies of speech visible. At last you could actually "see" what was going on. This was thought to be a greater advance than it actually turned out to be. Our thinking is strongly influenced by figures of speech. "Seeing is believing," even though when one is dealing with speech it is pretty obvious that hearing is what counts in the end. Nevertheless, the invention of the sound spectrograph was a great spur to research, and a result

of several years work at the Haskins Laboratories in New York during the 1950s
was a set of "minimal rules for synthesizing speech." These showed how stylized
formant patterns could generate the clues necessary to identify vowels and consonants.

The Haskins rules have formed the basis of many speech synthesis-by-rule
systems in the past three decades. A synthesis-by-rule system is a computer program whose input is a phonetic transcription of the utterance, and whose output
is a set of parameter tracks for a hardware synthesizer which then produces a
spoken version of it. The phonetic transcription may be broad or narrow,
depending on the system. Experience has shown that the Haskins rules really
are "minimal"—which is all they claimed to be. The success of a synthesis-by-
rule program depends on a vast collection of tiny details, each seemingly insignificant in isolation but whose effects combine to influence the speech quality
dramatically. The best current systems produce clearly understandable speech
that is still something of a strain to listen to for long periods of time. Most are
not so good, however, and some are absolutely awful. In recent times commercial influences have unfortunately restricted the free exchange of results and programs between academic researchers, thus slowing down progress. Research
attention has turned to prosodic factors, which are certainly less well understood
than segmental ones, and to synthesis from plain English text rather than from
phonetic transcriptions.

The remainder of this chapter describes the techniques of speech synthesis-
by-rule, from the point of view of joining phonemes together. The vital prosodic questions are left to the next chapter. But first you will have to learn
something about acoustic phonetics.

3.4. THE ACOUSTIC NATURE OF PHONEMES

Shortly after the invention of the sound spectrograph an inverse instrument was
developed, called the "pattern playback" synthesizer. The input to this was a
spectrogram, either in its original form or painted by hand, and it produced
speech sounds corresponding to the spectrogram. The pattern playback
synthesizer contained about fifty oscillators, each producing a component at a
different frequency. An optical arrangement was used to control the amplitude
of these by the lightness or darkness of each point on the frequency axis of the
spectrogram. As the spectrogram was drawn past the playing head, sound was
produced which had approximately the same frequency components as those
shown on it. However, the fundamental frequency was constant.

This machine allowed the complicated acoustic effects seen on a spectrogram, like those in Figures 1.4 and 1.5, to be replayed in either original or sim-
plified form. By doing this you could isolate the features which are important
for perception of the different sounds. The procedure was to copy from an
actual spectrogram the features which were most noticeable visually, and then to

make further changes by trial and error until the result was judged to have reasonable intelligibility when replayed.

For the purpose of trying to discover just what acoustic features give a particular phoneme its sound character, it is useful to consider the central, steady-state part separately from transitions into and out of the segment. The steady-state part is that sound which is heard when the phoneme is prolonged. The term *phoneme* is being used in a rather loose sense here: it is more appropriate to think of a *sound segment* rather than the abstract, language-dependent, unit which was introduced in Chapter 1. This is what I will call it.

Some sound segments can be recognized on the basis of their steady states alone. If you say any vowel, for example, and prolong it, there is no difficulty in identifying it by listening to any part of the utterance. This is not true for diphthongs. If you say "I" very slowly and freeze your vocal tract posture at any time, the resulting steady-state sound will not be enough to identify the diphthong. Instead, it will be a vowel somewhere between *aa* in "had" or *ar* in "hard," and *ee* in "heed." The same thing holds for glides. If you prolong the *w* in "want" or the *y* in "you," you will get a vowel resembling the *u* in "hood" or the *ee* in "heed." Fricatives, voiced or unvoiced, can be identified from the steady state. Stops cannot, for their steady state is silent.

Segments which you can recognize from their steady state are easy to synthesize. The difficulty lies with the others, for it must be the transitions from one to the next which carry the information. Thus "transitions" are an essential part of speech, and perhaps the word is unfortunate, for it calls to mind an unimportant bridge between one segment and the next.

We have now identified two categories of phoneme; ones which can be recognized from their steady state alone and ones for which transitional information is needed. We will call them *steady-state* and *transient* segments. The second term is not particularly appropriate, for even sounds in this class *can* be prolonged. The point is that the identifying information is in the transitions rather than the steady state.

3.4.1. Steady-State Segments

Table 3.2 shows suitable values for the formant parameters and excitation sources of a formant synthesizer, for steady-state segments only. All the frequencies involved obviously depend upon the speaker—the vocal tract size, accent, and speaking habits. The values given are nominal ones for a male speaker with a dialect of British English called "received pronunciation"—for it is what used to be "received" on the wireless in the old days before the British Broadcasting Corporation adopted a policy of more informal, more regional speech. Female speakers have formant frequencies approximately 15 percent higher than male ones.

The third formant is relatively unimportant for vowel identification. It is the first and second that give the vowels their character. Formant values for *h* are not given at all, for they would be meaningless. Although it is certainly a steady-state sound, *h* changes radically in context. If you say "had," "heed,"

TABLE 3.2 FORMANT SYNTHESIZER PARAMETERS FOR STEADY-STATE SOUNDS

		Excitation	Formant resonance frequencies (Hz)			Fricative resonance (Hz)
uh	(the)	voicing	500	1500	2500	
a	(bud)	voicing	700	1250	2550	
e	(head)	voicing	550	1950	2650	
i	(hid)	voicing	350	2100	2700	
o	(hod)	voicing	600	900	2600	
u	(hood)	voicing	400	950	2450	
aa	(had)	voicing	750	1750	2600	
ee	(heed)	voicing	300	2250	3100	
er	(heard)	voicing	600	1400	2450	
ar	(hard)	voicing	700	1100	2550	
aw	(hoard)	voicing	450	750	2650	
uu	(food)	voicing	300	950	2300	
h	(he)	aspiration				
s	(sin)	frication				6000
z	(zed)	frication and voicing				6000
sh	(shin)	frication				2300
zh	(vision)	frication and voicing				2300
f	(fin)	frication				4000
v	(vat)	frication and voicing				4000
th	(thin)	frication				5000
dh	(that)	frication and voicing				5000

"hud," and so on, and freeze your vocal tract posture on the initial h, you will find it already configured for the following vowel, in anticipation of it.

Amplitude values sometimes help you to identify phonemes, particularly for fricatives. The fricative th is the weakest sound, closely followed by f, with s and sh the strongest. You need a reasonable mix of voicing and frication amplitudes in the voiced fricatives. Their voicing amplitude is considerably less than in vowels.

There are other sounds that might be considered steady-state ones. You can probably identify m, n, and ng just by their steady states. However, the difference is not particularly strong, and it is the transitional parts which discriminate most effectively between these sounds. The steady state of r is quite distinctive, too, for most speakers, because the tip of the tongue is curled back in a so-called "retroflex" action, and this causes a radical change in the third formant resonance.

3.4.2. Transient Segments   Transient sounds include diphthongs, glides, nasals, voiced and unvoiced stops, and affricates. The first two are relatively easy to deal with, for they are basically continuous, gradual transitions from one vocal tract posture to another—sort of dynamic vowels. Diphthongs and

glides are similar to each other. In fact, "you" could be transcribed as a triph-
thong, *i e uu*, except that in the initial posture the tongue is even higher, and
the vocal tract correspondingly more constricted, than for the *i* in "hid"—
though not as constricted as in *sh*. Diphthongs and glides can be represented in
terms of "target" formant values. The idea is that the formant frequencies
move steadily from their initial values to their final ones. Of course, it is this
very *motion* that gives these phonemes their character. You cannot expect to
hear the phoneme if you simply prolong its target formant frequencies.

In nasals, there is a steady-state part with a strong nasal formant at a
fairly low frequency, because of the large size of the combined nasal and oral
cavity which is resonating. Higher formants are relatively weak, because all of
the sound comes out your nose and gets severely attenuated on its way. Transitions into and out of nasals are strongly nasalized, in the sense that the nasal
formant is there because the oral and nasal tracts are operating together. So in
fact are adjacent vowel segments. Whenever a sound becomes nasalized, the
formants move very rapidly from their previous positions into the new nasal
ones. This is because the velum acts as a switch, switching the nasal cavity in
and out very quickly. It turns out that almost *any* fast formant transition
sounds like a nasal, because your speech perception mechanisms are accustomed
to hearing them only in that context. This contrasts with the rather slow transitions in diphthongs and glides.

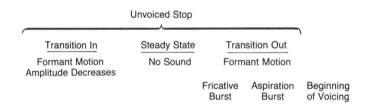

Figure 3.4 Sequence of events in an unvoiced stop.

Stops form the most complicated category of speech sounds. Consider
unvoiced stops first. They each have the three phases shown in Figure 3.4:
transition in, silent steady-state central portion, and transition out. There is a
lot of action on the transition out, and you could divide this part alone into
several phases. First, as the sound is released, there is a small burst of fricative
noise. Say "t t t ..." as in "tut-tut," without producing any voicing. A short
fricative resembling a very tiny *s* can be heard as the tongue leaves the roof of
the mouth. Frication is produced when the gap is very narrow, and ceases rapidly as it becomes wider. Next, when the sound is released at the end of an
unvoiced stop, a significant amount of aspiration follows after the release. Say
"pot," "tot," "cot" with force, and you will hear the *h*-like aspiration near the
beginning quite clearly. It doesn't always occur, though. You will hear no

aspiration when an *s* precedes the stop in the same syllable, as in "spot," "scot." The aspiration is what would distinguish "white spot" from the rather unlikely "White's pot." It tends to increase as the emphasis on the syllable increases, and this is an example of a prosodic feature influencing segmental characteristics. Finally, at the end of the segment, the aspiration—if any—will turn to voicing.

What has been described applies to *all* unvoiced stops. How do you tell one from another? The tiny fricative burst will be different because the noise is produced at different places in the vocal tract—at the lips for *p*, tongue and front of palate for *t*, and tongue and back of palate for *k*. The most important difference, however, is the formant motion illuminated by the last vestiges of voicing at the beginning of the stop, and by both aspiration and the onset of voicing at the end. Each stop has target formant values which affect the transitions in and out, even though they cannot be heard during the stopped portion, for there is no sound there. An added complexity is that the target positions themselves vary to some extent, depending on the adjacent segments. If the stop is heavily aspirated, the vocal tract will almost have reached its shape for the following vowel before voicing begins, but the formant transitions will still be perceived because they affect the sound quality of aspiration.

The voiced stops *b*, *d*, and *g* are quite similar to their unvoiced analogs *p*, *t*, and *k*. You can tell them from one another by the formant transitions to target positions, heard at the beginning and end of the sound segment. You can tell them from their unvoiced counterparts by the fact that more voicing is present: It lingers on longer at the beginning and commences earlier at the end. Unlike unvoiced stops, there is little or no aspiration at the end. If an unvoiced stop is uttered in a context where aspiration is suppressed, as in "spot," it is almost identical to the corresponding voiced stop, "sbot." Luckily no words in English require us to make a distinction in such contexts. Voicing sometimes continues through the entire stopped portion of a voiced stop, especially when it is surrounded by other voiced segments. When saying a word like "baby" slowly, you can choose whether or not to prolong voicing throughout the second *b*. If you do, it is at quite a low amplitude because your lips are closed and the sound escapes through your cheeks. Try doing it for a very long time and your cheeks will fill up with air. This makes the whole sound very weak, and in particular severely attenuates high-frequency components. It can be simulated with a weak first formant at a low resonant frequency. The effect can easily be seen on a spectrogram, and is known as a *voice bar*. The phases of a voiced stop are summarized in Figure 3.5.

There are many variations of stops that have not been mentioned. In a phrase like "good news," nasal plosion occurs between the *d* and the *n*. You can feel this when you say it. The nasal formant appears in anticipation of the nasal, at the end of the *d*. Stop bursts are often suppressed when the next sound is a stop too. The burst on the *p* of "apt" is an example of this. It is difficult to distinguish a voiced stop from an unvoiced one at the end of a

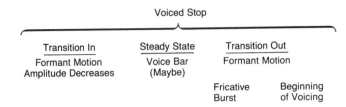

Figure 3.5 Sequence of events in a voiced stop.

word. For example, it is hard to make "cab" different from "cap." If you are trying to make yourself particularly clear you will put a short neutral vowel after the voiced stop to emphasize its early onset of voicing. Italians generally do this anyway, for it is the norm in their own language. Do it all the time and you will sound as though you are imitating an Italian.

Finally, we turn to affricates. There are only two in English, and they are relatively rare: *ch* as in "chin" and *j* as in "djinn." They are very similar to the stops *t* and *d* followed by the fricatives *sh* and *zh* respectively, and you can simulate them quite effectively just by producing the appropriate phoneme pair. The affricate *ch* has a closing phase, a stopped phase, and a long fricative burst. There is no aspiration, for the vocal cords are not involved. The affricate *j* is the same except that voicing extends further into the stopped portion, and the terminating fricative is also voiced. It may be pronounced with a voice bar if the preceding segment is voiced, as in "adjunct."

3.5. SPEECH SYNTHESIS BY RULE

Generation of speech by rules which act upon a phonetic transcription was first investigated in the early 1960s. Most systems employ a hardware synthesizer to reduce the load on the computer which operates the rules. The speech-by-rule program, rather than the synthesizer, is almost always the weak link in the chain. Formant synthesizers are popular for speech-by-rule systems, but parameter tracks for a formant synthesizer can easily be converted into linear prediction parameters, and systems are beginning to appear which use linear predictive synthesizers.

The phrase *synthesis by rule*, which people often use, does not make it clear just what sort of things the rules are supposed to do, and what information must be included explicitly in the input transcription. Early systems made no attempt at all to simulate prosodics. Pitch and rhythm could usually be controlled, but only by the tedious process of inserting pitch and duration numbers for each phoneme in the input. Some kind of prosodic control was often incorporated later, but usually as a completely separate phase from segmental synthesis. This does not allow interaction effects, such as the above-mentioned extra aspiration for voiceless stops in accented syllables, to be taken into account. Even systems which perform prosodic operations invariably need to have specifications embedded in the input to give some description of what the intonation should be and where the stressed syllables are. We will describe such specifications in the next chapter.

Turning a phonetic transcription of an utterance into parameter tracks for a synthesizer is a process of data *expansion*. Six bits are enough to specify a phoneme, since there are less than forty in the language, and $2^6 = 64$. Your normal speaking rate is probably in the region of twelve phonemes per second. This leads to an input data rate of about 72 bit/s. The data rate required to control the synthesizer will depend upon the number of parameters and the rate at which they are sampled. As we saw in the last chapter, a typical figure is 1.2 Kbit/s. Hence something approaching a fifty-fold data expansion is involved.

Figure 3.6 shows the parameter tracks for a formant synthesizer like Computalker saying the utterance *s i k s* (six). There are eight parameters. If you look at parameter 5 you can see the onset of frication at the beginning and end, and parameter 1 shows the amplitude of voicing come on for the *i* and off again before the *k*. The pitch, parameter 0, is falling slowly throughout the utterance. These tracks are stylized: They come from a computer synthesis-by-rule program and not from a human utterance. With a parameter update interval of 10 ms, the graphs can be represented by 90 sets of eight parameter values, a total of 720 values or 4320 bits if six bits are used for each value. Contrast this with the input of only four phoneme segments, or say 24 bits.

3.5.1. A Segment-by-Segment System

In 1964, the first comprehensive implementation of a computer-based synthesis-by-rule system was constructed. The same system is still in use today, although it has been reworked in a more modern form. The inventory of sound segments includes the phonemes listed in Table 1.1, as well as diphthongs. Some phonemes are expanded into subphonemic "phases" by the program. Stops have three phases, corresponding to the closing part, the silent steady state, and the opening part at the end of the stop. Diphthongs have two phases. We will call individual phases and single-phase phonemes *segments*, for exactly the same transition rules apply to each.

As you can see in Figure 3.6, each parameter track is constructed from straight-line pieces. There are no curves. Consider a pair of adjacent segments in an utterance to be synthesized. The program gives each one a steady-state portion and an internal transition. Thus going from one to another we will get the first phoneme's steady state, its internal transition, the second phoneme's internal transition, and finally its steady state, in sequence. The internal transition of one phoneme is called *external* as far as the other is concerned. This is important because instead of each segment's being responsible for its own

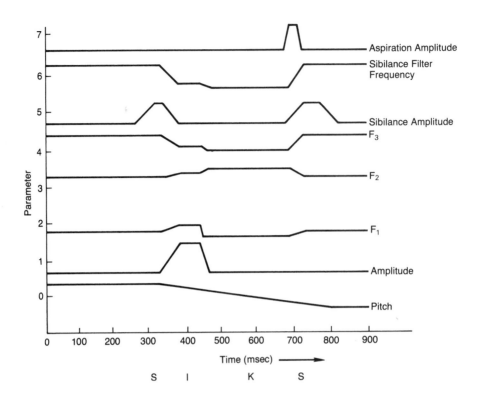

Figure 3.6   Parameter tracks for a synthesizer saying   *s i k s*.

internal transition, one of the pair is identified as "dominant," and it controls the duration of both transitions—its internal one and its external (the other's internal) one. For example, in Figure 3.7 the segment *sh* dominates *ee*, and so it governs the duration of both transitions shown. Note that each segment contributes as many as three straight-line pieces to the parameter track.

The notion of domination is similar to that mentioned earlier for joining words. There we said that it might be a good idea, in smoothing the parameter values between two words, to load the average in favor of the word whose spectrum is changing more quickly. The difference is that whereas previously the dominant segment was identified by looking at the spectrums of both, here we rank segments according to a precedence list, and the higher-ranking one dominates. But the same general principle applies, for segments of stop consonants have the highest rank and also the quickest change in spectrum, while fricatives, nasals, glides, and vowels follow in that order.

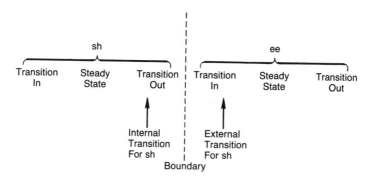

Figure 3.7 Internal and external transitions between two segments.

The joining procedure is controlled by a table which contains 25 quantities for each segment. The rank is stored so that you, or, more correctly, the computer program, can find out which segment dominates each pair. There are two overall durations, for stressed and unstressed occurrences of the phoneme. Transition durations are given separately for internal and external transitions of formant frequencies and amplitudes. There are eight target parameter values; the amplitudes and frequencies of three formants, plus fricative information. Finally, a total of ten quantities specify how to calculate boundary values for formant frequencies and amplitudes.

This table is rather large. Although English has only around thirty-five phonemes, there are 80 segments in all, because many phonemes are represented by more than one segment. Hence it has $80 \times 25 = 2000$ entries. The system ran on what was then—1964—a large computer. It worked offline. You submitted your job, with the phonetic transcription punched on to paper tape, and maybe next day a paper tape came back which you could play through the synthesizer.

The advantage of such a large table of "rules" is the flexibility it gives. For example, transition durations are specified independently for formant frequency and amplitude parameters. This permits fine control, which is particularly useful for stops.

The total duration of each phoneme is specified in the input, by the person who prepares the utterance for the computer. So is the pitch, at various points in each phoneme. It could easily happen that the two transition durations which are calculated for a segment are actually bigger than the total duration specified for it. In this case, the steady-state target values will be approached but not actually attained. This simulates a situation where you begin to move your tongue towards a given position, but fail to reach it because another movement is started soon after.

3.5.2. An Event-Based System

The synthesis system described above, in common with many others, takes an uncompromisingly segment-by-segment view of speech. The next phoneme is read, perhaps split into a few segments, and these are synthesized one by one, with due attention being paid to transitions between them. Some later work uses a broader base—I mentioned above the move back to syllables as a basic unit for joining together. As time goes on, more and more people are abandoning the "segmental assumption" that progress through the utterance should be made one segment at a time, in favor of a description of speech based upon perceptually relevant "events." This new framework is interesting because it provides an opportunity for prosodic considerations to be treated as an integral part of the synthesis process.

The phonetic segments and other information that specify an utterance can be regarded as a list of events which describes it at a relatively high level. The list contains information like "Start phoneme p." It is a high-level description, because this single entry actually causes several things to happen, in the mouth as you speak, or in the acoustic waveform as you listen. Synthesis-by-rule is the act of taking this list and elaborating on it to produce lower-level events which are realized by the vocal tract, or acoustically simulated by a formant or linear predictive synthesizer, to give a speech waveform. In articulatory terms, an event might be "Begin tongue motion towards upper teeth with a given effort," while in formant terms it could be "Begin second formant transition toward 1500 Hz at a given rate." (These two examples are for illustration only, and are *not* intended to describe the same event. A tongue motion causes much more than the transition of a single formant.) The influences of one phoneme on another, such as when stop bursts are suppressed or nasalized, should be easier to imitate within an event-based scheme than in a segment-to-segment one.

The system we look at now, called ISP, is event-based. The key to its operation is the *synthesis list*. To prepare an utterance for synthesis, the phoneme names and so on which specify it are joined into a linked list. Figure 3.8 shows the start of the list created for the input

$$1 \quad dh \; i \; z \quad i \; z \quad /*d \; zh \; aa \; k \; s \quad /h \; aa \; u \; s$$

or "This is Jack's house." The "1 ... /* ... / ..." are prosodic markers which will be discussed in the next chapter. Once the list has been created, it is transformed by computer programs which link new elements into the list and remove ones that are no longer needed. For example, rhythm and pitch programs add in syllable boundaries and duration and pitch specifications. The segmental synthesis program also links events into appropriate places in the list. As it proceeds, any elements which are no longer useful are removed. Each event has a time at which it becomes due. The computer program which handles the speech synthesizer removes events from the list at the appropriate times and uses them to control the hardware device.

Each list element has a pointer which indicates the next element of the list, and five data words. Several kinds of things may appear in the original input,

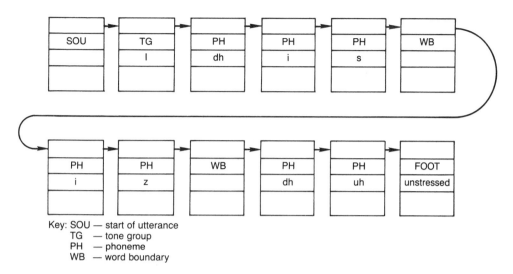

Key: SOU — start of utterance
     TG — tone group
     PH — phoneme
     WB — word boundary

Figure 3.8 Start of an ISP synthesis list.

and the first data word shows what type of element it is. For example, punctuation indicates a short pause. Intonation and rhythm indicators like the "1,"
"/," and "/*" in the example above may appear. Phoneme segments themselves are another kind of element. Syllable boundaries may be shown explicitly
in the input by an apostrophe, and pitch or duration information for individual
phonemes may also be put in if you wish.

Several of these have to do with prosodic features. A great advantage of
the structure is that it does not create an artificial division between segmentals
and prosody. Syllable boundaries and duration and pitch information are
optional. You can specify them in the input if you want, but if not, they will
be computed for you by the program. This gives you a natural way to override
decisions taken by the program if you think they are wrong.

As synthesis proceeds, new elements are linked into the synthesis list. For
segmental purposes, three types of event are defined: target events, increment
events, and aspiration events. A target event says, in effect, "At time . . .,
parameter number . . . should begin to move towards a value . . ., to reach it at
time . . . ." Here, " . . ." indicates a data value which is stored as part of that
event: the time when it becomes due, the parameter which it affects, the target
value of that parameter, and the duration of the event. When the time comes,
motion of the parameter towards the target is begun. If no other event inter-
venes, the target value will be reached after the given time duration has elapsed.
However, another target event for the parameter may change its motion before
the target has been attained. Increment events specify a temporary increase in
the value of a parameter. As well as the time when the event becomes due,

they contain a parameter number, a parameter increment, and a time duration. The fixed increment is added to the parameter value throughout the duration specified. This provides an easy way to make a fricative burst during the opening phase of a stop consonant. Aspiration events switch the mode of excitation from voicing to aspiration for a given period of time. This makes it easy to simulate the aspirated part of an unvoiced stop by simply changing from voicing to aspiration for the duration of the event.

TABLE 3.3   RULE TABLE FOR AN EVENT-BASED SYNTHESIS-BY-RULE PROGRAM

	Excitation	Formant resonance frequencies (Hz)			Fricative resonance (Hz)	Type
uh	voicing	490	1480	2500		vowel
a	voicing	720	1240	2540		vowel
e	voicing	560	1970	2640		vowel
i	voicing	360	2100	2700		vowel
o	voicing	600	890	2600		vowel
u	voicing	380	950	2440		vowel
aa	voicing	750	1750	2600		vowel
ee	voicing	290	2270	3090		long vowel
er	voicing	580	1380	2440		long vowel
ar	voicing	680	1080	2540		long vowel
aw	voicing	450	740	2640		long vowel
uu	voicing	310	940	2320		long vowel
h	aspiration					h
r	voicing	240	1190	1550		glide
w	voicing	240	650			glide
l	voicing	380	1190			glide
y	voicing	240	2270			glide
m	voicing	190	690	2000		nasal
b	none	100	690	2000		stop
p	none	100	690	2000		stop
n	voicing	190	1780	3300		nasal
d	none	100	1780	3300		stop
t	none	100	1780	3300		stop
ng	voicing	190	2300	2500		nasal
g	none	100	2300	2500		stop
k	none	100	2300	2500		stop
s	frication				6000	fricative
z	frication and voicing	190	1780	3300	6000	fricative
sh	frication				2300	fricative
zh	frication and voicing	190	2120	2700	2300	fricative
f	frication				4000	fricative
v	frication and voicing	190	690	3300	4000	fricative
th	frication				5000	fricative
dh	frication and voicing	190	1780	3300	5000	fricative

The rule table for this system is shown in Table 3.3. It holds target positions for each phoneme segment, as well as the segment type. The segment type is used to trigger events by computer procedures which can examine the context of the segment. In principle, this allows the synthesis to be considerably more sophisticated than a simple segment-by-segment approach.

For example, Table 3.4 summarizes some of the subtleties of the speech production process which have been mentioned earlier in this chapter. Most of them depend critically on the context of a segment. The prosodic context, like whether two segments are in the same syllable, or whether a syllable is stressed, is important, too. A scheme where data-dependent "demons" fire on particular patterns in a linked list seems to be a sensible way to incorporate such rules.

TABLE 3.4   SOME WAYS IN WHICH A PHONEME
CAN INFLUENCE ITS NEIGHBORS

Fricative bursts on stops
Aspiration bursts on unvoiced stops, affected by
        preceding consonant in this syllable (suppress burst if fricative)
        following consonant (suppress burst if another stop; introduce
            nasal plosion if a nasal)
        prosodics (increase burst if syllable is stressed)
Voice bar on voiced stops (in intervocalic position)
Post-voicing on final voiced stops, if syllable is stressed
Anticipation of the next vocal posture, for *h*
Vowel coloring when a nasal or glide follows

3.6. DISCUSSION

There are two opposing trends in speech synthesis by rule. On the one hand, larger and larger segment inventories can be used, containing more and more variants of phonemes explicitly. This is the approach of the Votrax sound-segment synthesizer, discussed in the last chapter. It makes it difficult for you to prepare something for the computer to say, because you have to decide which of the many alternatives to use for each phoneme. On the other hand, the segment inventory can be kept small, perhaps just the phonemes as in the ISP system. Then the computer program has to decide on how to vary the sound quality and articulation of each phoneme. To do so it must know about the segmental and prosodic context. An event-based approach seems to give the best chance of allowing segments to be modified according to their context.

An event-based system would be an ideal way of implementing a high-level model of the vocal tract for speech synthesis by rule. It would be much more satisfying to have the rule table contain articulatory target positions instead of formant frequencies, with events like "Begin tongue motion towards upper teeth with a given effort." The problem is that hard data on articulatory postures and constraints is much more difficult to gather than formant and amplitude information.

3.7. FURTHER READING

Fry, D.B., ed., *Acoustic Phonetics*. Cambridge, England: Cambridge University Press, 1976. This book of readings contains many classic papers on acoustic phonetics published from 1922 to 1965. It covers much of the history of the subject, and is intended primarily for students of linguistics.

Lehiste, I., ed., *Readings in Acoustic Phonetics*. Cambridge, Massachusetts: MIT Press, 1967. Another basic collection of references which covers much the same ground as Fry's book above.

Potter, R.K., G.A. Kopp, and H.C. Green, *Visible Speech*. New York: Van Nostrand, 1947. This book introduced the sound spectrogram and its use. It gives an interesting insight into the euphoria that people felt when they first realized that the features of speech could be examined visually. Don't forget, though, that experience since the book was published has indicated that to be able to *see* the features of speech is not such a great advance after all—it's hearing that counts in the end!

4

The Utterance Level: Intonation and Text

You often hear people say things like "It's not what they said, it's the way that they said it," or "Don't speak to me in that tone of voice." It is the so-called *prosodic* features of the speech that make up the "tone of voice." Now that you have seen how to produce a speech waveform, and how to join segments together, it's time to move up to these higher-level features and see how they can be simulated. This raises the very interesting question of how the desired "tone of voice" should be communicated to the speech synthesis system. Ideally, perhaps, the system should read plain text—just as a person does. But then, you see, it would have to *understand* the text first, for everyone knows that you can't make a good job of reading aloud unless you understand what you are reading. We will look later at what this means, and it will lead us into deep water, for no one really knows very much about machine "understanding."

Prosodic features are ones which affect an utterance as a whole, rather than having a local influence on individual sound segments. For example, whether your voicing continues right through the second *b* of "baby" or whether you leave a stop gap is a segmental question, not a prosodic one. If you find it hard to tell the difference between a machine's *t*s and its *d*s, then it has a segmental problem, not a prosodic one. But if it speaks in an unnatural, grating, monotone—as simulated robots often do in movies and on TV—then it is the prosodic features that are at fault. Or if the rhythm sounds odd, so that some syllables are drawn out longer than they should be and others sound too choppy, or if you thought it said "baby!" and it should have said "baby?" then these are prosodic problems.

The most important prosodic feature is pitch, or intonation. This is how you often distinguish a question from a command, and is a large part of how you display emotions such as surprise, sadness, and anger. The next most important is rhythm. Between them, pitch and rhythm give the important quality of *stress*—a rather vaguely defined word that means different things to different people. We will discuss these features in the next section. Surprisingly, loudness—an obviously prosodic feature—isn't as important as you might think. You *don't* stress things effectively just by saying them louder, as anyone with small children will confirm!

Let's recognize at the outset that prosodics and segmentals are very closely intertwined. Pitch is largely a prosodic feature, yet short-term variations in it do in fact help to clarify voiced stop consonants. Loudness, which is also mainly prosodic, affects the identification of fricatives. The rhythm of speech, another prosodic feature, is highlighted by changes in vowel quality which occur at the segmental level. You can't separate the two kinds of features completely. The essential difference is that prosodics have to do with global aspects of a significant stretch of speech, while segmentals are purely local to a small group of phonemes.

I have tried to emphasize throughout this book that prosodic features are important in speech synthesis. There is something very basic about them. Rhythm is an essential part of all bodily activity—of breathing, walking, and making love—so it pervades speech too. Mothers and babies communicate effectively using intonation alone. Some experiments have indicated that the language environment of infants affects their babbling at an early age, before they can articulate words properly. There is no doubt that "tone of voice" plays a large part in human communication.

Early attempts at synthesis didn't pay very much attention to prosodics. Perhaps it was thought enough to get the words across by providing clear segmentals. As artificial speech grows more widespread, however, it seems clear that it won't be acceptable to the man in the street unless it has natural-sounding prosodics. You may be able to understand flat, unrhythmical speech in short stretches, but it strains your concentration when you have to listen to a lot of it. Unfortunately, current commercial speech output systems do not really tackle prosodic questions. Indeed, our present knowledge of them is rather inadequate.

The synthesis of prosodic features is a difficult and controversial area, and the problem of how to glean the necessary information from text is not really understood at all. That gives this chapter a rather different flavor from the others. It's hard to be definite about alternative strategies and methods. In order to be as concrete and down-to-earth as possible, I will describe as examples two methods of prosodic synthesis. The first copies natural pitch from one utterance to another, while the second shows how timing and pitch, which are completely artificial, can be used in synthetic speech.

As part of the second example, we will look at a notation for describing prosodic features to a computer. This notation is substantially the same as that used by linguists when recording natural utterances. What we turn to next is whether you can generate this information, or at least some of it, from text. The chief problem here is that before you can decide on what sort of intonation pattern to use, you first have to settle on an "interpretation" of the text. This interpretation will depend on the meaning, on your attitude to what you are saying, and your expectations of your listener's reaction too.

The other problem in working from plain text is that pronunciation rules must be used to turn the English into a phonetic transcription suitable for the synthesis-by-rule procedures described in the last chapter. In the final section we look at a simple pronunciation program which works surprisingly well.

4.1. WHAT IS STRESS?

Everyone knows what "stress" means in language. When listening to natural speech, we would probably agree on which syllables are stressed. From the speaker's point of view, a stressed syllable is produced by pushing more air out of the lungs. For a listener, the points of stress are "obvious."

It is surprisingly difficult to say, in acoustic terms, what it is that makes a syllable stressed. You may think that stressed syllables are louder than the others. Measurements, however, show that this is not necessarily—nor even usually—so. Stressed syllables often have a longer vowel than unstressed ones—but often they don't. If you say "little" or "bigger" you will find that the vowel in the first, stressed syllable is short and shows little sign of lengthening as you increase the emphasis. Indeed, experiments using two-syllable nonsense words have shown that some people consistently judge the *shorter* syllable to be stressed, other things being equal. Pitch often helps to indicate stress. It's not that stressed syllables always have a higher or lower pitch than others, or even that they are uttered with a rising or falling intonation. It is the *rate of change* of pitch that tends to be greater for stressed syllables. A sharp rise or fall, or a reversal of direction, helps to give emphasis.

Another complicating factor is that certain *segmental* changes have a definite effect on the perception of stress. We saw in the last chapter that unvoiced stops at the beginning of a syllable have extra aspiration if they are stressed. (Try it with a stressed "pit" or "pot.") Also, because stressed syllables are spoken with greater effort than others, the formant transitions are more likely to reach their target values under circumstances where they would otherwise fall short. In unstressed syllables, vowels like *ee*, *aa*, *uu* that involve extreme tongue positions move to more relaxed, neutral ones like *i*, *uh*, and *u* respectively. Vowels in unstressed syllables often become "reduced" into a centralized form. Look at these examples:

diplomat	*d i p l uh m aa t*
diplomacy	*d i p l uh u m uh s i*
diplomatic	*d i p l uh m aa t i k*

The vowel of the second syllable is reduced to *uh* in "diplomat" and "diplomatic," whereas the root form "diploma," and also "diplomacy," have the diphthong *uh u* there. The third syllable has an *aa* in "diplomat" and "diplomatic" which is reduced to *uh* in "diplomacy." In these cases the reduction is shown explicitly in the phonetic transcription, but in more marginal examples where it is less extreme it may not be.

Acoustically, then, stress is indicated by the prosodic features of timing and pitch, and to a much lesser extent by loudness. It is also accompanied by *segmental* changes that stem from greater vocal effort and hence clearer articulation. It is a rather subtle feature that certainly doesn't correspond simply to duration increases or pitch rises. It seems that you unconsciously put together all the clues that are present in an utterance in order to deduce which syllables are stressed.

The situation is confused by the fact that some syllables in words are often said in ordinary language to be "stressed" on account of their position in the word. In the example words above we talked about which syllable the stress was on. But stress is really *latent* in the indicated syllables and only is made manifest when they are spoken, and then to a greater or lesser degree depending on exactly how they are spoken.

Nonstandard stress patterns are often used to bring out contrasts. Words like "a" and "the" are normally unstressed, but can be emphasized in contexts where ambiguity has arisen. This means that you must consider quite sophisticated factors when deciding where to place the stress. These include the grammar and meaning of the utterance, as well as the attitude of the speaker and the likely reaction of the listener. For example, I might say

"Anna *and* Nikki should go"

with emphasis on the "and" purely because I was aware that you might not want to send them both—perhaps you might feel that the effect on the recipient would be devastating! Clearly the synthesis program needs somehow to be able to tell how the sentence is supposed to be spoken.

4.2. COPYING PITCH FROM ONE UTTERANCE TO ANOTHER

We looked in the last chapter at how you can record utterances that depend on variable data and slot in the appropriate data words when the time comes to speak. For example, if messages are constructed from templates like

Your car is booked for ... days from ... on the ... of ...

it is nice to be able to store the pitch of one complete instance of the message and apply it to all synthetic versions. This will be possible only if the speech is stored in a way which factors out the pitch into a separate parameter track. You can't do it if just the raw digitized waveform is stored. But you can if the speech is generated by a linear predictive or formant synthesizer.

Take the system mentioned earlier which generated seven-digit telephone numbers by joining together words using a formant synthesizer. In it, a single natural pitch pattern was applied to all utterances. It was chosen to match as closely as possible the general shape of the pitch measured in naturally spoken telephone numbers. This was quite easy, because telephone numbers have hardly any variety in the sequence of stressed and unstressed syllables. The only digit which has more than one syllable is "seven." Significant problems arise when more general utterances are considered.

Suppose the pitch of one utterance, which I will call the "source," is to be transferred to another, the "target." The source is recorded complete with its natural pitch. But the target has been constructed by filling slots in templates with separately recorded words. Assume that both utterances are encoded in a way which makes the pitch a separate parameter. Then there are no technical obstacles to combining the pitch track of one utterance with the other parameters of a different one.

To be quite specific, we will look at a procedure for transferring pitch between messages of the form

The price is ... dollars and ... cents

where the slots are filled by numbers less than 100; and of the form

The price is ... cents

The different possible prices include a wide range of syllable configurations. Since the numbers are restricted to be less than 100, there could be as few as one syllable in the variable part, if the number is "2," or as many as five if it is "77"—count them! The messages all convey the same sort of information, so it is reasonable to synthesize them in the same tone of voice.

It is essential to take into account the configuration of syllables so that pitch is transferred between corresponding syllables rather than over the utterance as a whole. Fortunately, syllable boundaries can be detected automatically with a fair degree of accuracy, especially if the speaker enunciates words carefully. This means that we don't have to go through the tedious process of marking by hand the syllable boundaries for everything in the dictionary.

If the source and target utterances have the same number of syllables, and the same pattern of stressed and unstressed syllables, pitch can simply be transferred from a syllable in the source to the corresponding one in the target. But if the pattern differs—even though the number of syllables may be the same, as in "eleven" and "seventeen"—then a simple one-to-one mapping will conflict with the stress points, and will certainly sound unnatural. In these cases you have to ensure that the pitch is mapped in a plausible way. The rules which follow seem to give reasonable results in most cases.

The syllables of each utterance can be classified as "stressed" and "unstressed." In our example, the sentences have fixed "carrier" parts and variable "number" parts. The carrier syllables are

The price is . . . dollars and . . . cents

Of these, three syllables are stressed, namely

. . . price . . . dol − . . . cents

They should be marked to make it easier to align the source and target syllables properly. Also, the stressed syllables in the variable "number" parts should be marked. Even then, it may still be difficult to decide on how the target syllables should correspond with those of the source. This is because the pattern of stressed and unstressed syllables may be different in the two utterances.

The simplest case is when the variable parts in both source and target have the same number of syllables, and the same pattern of stress. For example, with

[source]   The price is twenty cents

[target   The price is seven cents

there is no problem. The pitch of "twen −" gets mapped directly on to "sev −," and than of "ty" on to "en." Syllables in the source which have no correspondence in the target can be ignored. In

[source]   The price is twenty cents

[target]   The price is two cents

"two" gets the pitch of "twen −," and that of "ty" is not used at all. If there are more syllables in the target than in the source, you have to replicate the pitch of the source for each additional syllable in the target. A stressed syllable should be selected for copying if the unmatched target syllable is stressed, and similarly for unstressed ones. For example, in

[source]   The price is twenty cents

[target]   The price is seventy cents

the "twen −" gets copied to the "sev −," and the "ty" to the "en −." Then the pitch on the "ty" must be replicated to serve the "ty" at the end of "seventy" as well. It is rather dangerous to copy exactly a part of a pitch pattern, for the ear is very sensitive to identical pitch variation on neighboring segments of speech. This is especially true when the segment is stressed. To avoid the problem, whenever the pitch on a stressed syllable is replicated, the pitch values should be decreased a little bit on the second copy. It sometimes happens that a single stressed syllable in the source needs to cover a stressed-unstressed pair in the target. In this case the first part of the source pitch track can be used for the stressed syllable, and the rest for the unstressed one.

The example of Figure 4.1 will help to make these rules clear. It shows the mapping

[source]   The price is forty-five dollars and three cents

[target]   The price is eleven dollars and forty-five cents

—quite a complicated example. The carrier syllables get mapped straight across from one utterance to the other. The stressed middle syllable of "eleven" gets its pitch from the first syllable of "forty-," which is also stressed. The last syllable of "eleven" gets its pitch from the last syllable of "forty-." But for the first, we have to steal the pitch from the "is," and replicate it, for we must use an unstressed syllable. Similarly, replication is used to map "three" on to "forty-five," one copy for the "forty-" and the other for the "five." Finally, to match the one syllable of "three" to the two of "forty-," we have to divide the pitch into two parts, using a nominal 70 percent $-$ 30 percent split. Note that you need to do only the marking by hand. These detailed mapping decisions can be left to the computer.

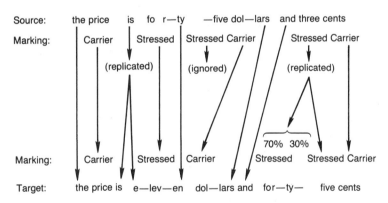

Figure 4.1 Example of the pitch transfer procedure.

Figure 4.2 shows the result of transferring the pitch from "The price is ten cents" to "The price is seventy-seven cents." You can see how the pitch on the last part of the "ten" has been used to cover the first "en" syllable, and it has been replicated to serve the "-ty" syllable also. The pitch on the second "seven" can be seen to be a copy of the first one, but a little lower. Notice, incidentally, that there is an artifact in the pitch: It is doubled on the final part of one of the "cents." This is actually quite common with automatic pitch extraction procedures.

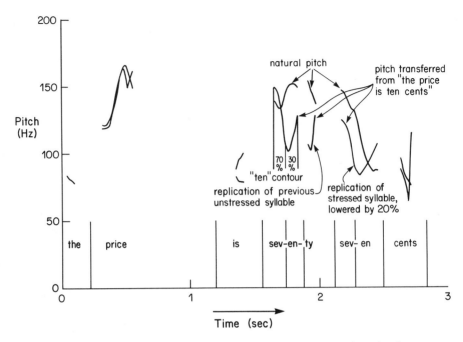

Figure 4.2 Pitch transferred from "the price is ten cents" to "the price is seventy-seven cents."

Some experiments have shown that this pitch transfer method works quite well on the kind of utterances we are considering. First, you can take two sentences where the speaker says the same words on different occasions. Then you can transfer the pitch from copy A to copy B, and vice versa. If you include resynthesized versions of the original sentences A and B, you get four different utterances. Although all four often sound extremely similar, sometimes the pitch of the two originals are quite different. Then it is immediately obvious to the ear that two of the four utterances have the same intonation, and that it is different from that shared by the other two. However, it is impossible to tell which two of the four utterances do not have their original intonation patterns.

In another experiment, the pitch was transferred between messages of the form "The price is . . . cents," which have only one variable part. With ten original sentences, each one can be regenerated with pitch transferred from each of the other nine. When you listen to them in pairs, one having its original pitch and the other with intonation transferred from some other utterance, it is sometimes obvious which one is "right." Just as often, however, you simply can't tell—even though the intonation may sound definitely different in each case.

When the utterances have two variable parts, as in "The price is . . . dollars and . . . cents," the results are significantly worse. Nevertheless, if you choose the source utterance carefully, you are still likely to be able to find an intonation which can be applied to all the target utterances without people being able to tell the originals.

All in all, the experiments show that the procedure can generate stereotyped, but different, utterances of high quality. It can handle different syllable patterns satisfactorily. However, if individual sentences contain several variable parts, the source utterance should be selected with the help of listening tests.

4.3. SYNTHETIC RHYTHM AND PITCH

The pitch transfer method can give good results for some fairly straightforward applications. But it treats complete utterances as a single unit, using slot-fillers to contain variable data, so it becomes unmanageable in situations where there is a large variety of utterances. When we encountered this problem in the last chapter in the context of joining segments together, we saw that the solution was to use smaller units—there are far fewer phonemes in English than there are words or sentences. But this is an approach that won't work with prosodic features, because they affect an utterance as a whole and so can't be broken up. What we need is a notation to describe the intonation and stress of each utterance.

The notation we will use is derived from one which was designed to help foreigners speak English. This emphasizes the fact that, unlike many other systems, it was designed for use by people, not just linguists. It has been incorporated into the ISP speech synthesis system which we met in the last chapter. Here are some examples of it:

```
3 ^ aw t uh/m aa t i k  /s in th uh s i s  uh v  /*s p ee t sh
1 ^ f r uh m  uh  f uh/*n e t i k  /r e p r uh z e n/t e i sh uh n
```

which reads "automatic synthesis of speech, from a phonetic representation."

In these examples, two different levels of stress are marked. The most forceful is called *tonic stress*, and is marked by "*" before the syllable. You might think of it as "sentence" stress, although in an actual sentence there may be more than one point of tonic stress. In fact, the example shows two in one sentence—one for each phrase. In English, we might write the example as "automatic synthesis of *speech*, from a *phonetic* representation," italicizing the points of sentence stress. The second kind of stress is called *foot stress*, and is marked by "/" before the syllable. The notion of a "foot" controls the rhythm of the speech in a way that will be described in a moment. You might think of it as "word" stress, although again there might be more than one in a long word like "*rep*resen*ta*tion," and there is usually none at all in a small, unimportant, word like "of" and "from." You might call no stress at all a third level, corresponding to syllables which are not specially marked. There is in fact yet another, fourth, level of stress. This operates at a *segmental* level and depends on the kind of vowel in the syllable. For example, the very first syllable of "automatic" is more prominent than the second, simply because it contains an extreme vowel, *aw*, while the second contains a centralized, reduced one, *uh*.

Utterances are divided by punctuation into *tone groups,* which are the basic prosodic unit. There are two in the example. They correspond roughly with short sentences or clauses. The shape of the pitch variation is governed by a number at the start of each tone group. Crude control over pauses is achieved by punctuation marks. A period, for example, signals a pause, whereas comma does not. Longer pauses can be obtained by several periods as in ".…" The "^" character means a so-called *silent stress* or breath point. Word boundaries are shown by two spaces between phonemes, and are sometimes important to decide on the rhythm of the syllables. As mentioned in the last chapter, syllable boundaries and explicit pitch and duration numbers can also be included in the input if you want. If they are not, the ISP system will attempt to compute them.

4.3.1. Rhythm
One starting point for imitating the rhythm of English speech is to assume that stresses recur at regular intervals. These stresses are primarily *rhythmic* ones, and are different from the tonic stress mentioned above, which is signaled mainly by *intonation*. Rhythmic stresses are shown in the notation by a "/." The stretch between one and the next is called a *foot*. The assumption that they recur at regular intervals is often called the hypothesis of isochronous feet: *isochronous* means "occupying equal time."

Although there is considerable controversy about whether this hypothesis is actually true, or even approximately true, for real speech, it has some advantages for speech synthesis. The rhythm of natural speech is influenced by many higher-level processes, like grammar and meaning, which are not very well understood. The use of feet provides a simple notation for representing the result of this higher-level processing which people find quite easy to grasp. Using isochronous feet, you get a heavily accentuated, but not unnatural, speech rhythm. This can easily be moderated into a more relaxed rhythm by departing from isochrony in a controlled manner.

The ISP procedure does not make feet exactly isochronous. It starts with a standard foot duration and tries to fit the syllables of the foot into this time. If this would squash some syllables up too much, the isochrony constraint is relaxed and the foot is expanded. The rate of talking is governed by the standard foot duration. If this is short, many feet will be forced to have durations longer than the standard, and the speech will be "less isochronous." This seems reasonable when you think of human speech. If the standard time is longer, however, the minimum syllable limit will always be exceeded and the speech will be completely isochronous.

People have often noticed that the final foot of an utterance tends to be longer than others. So does the tonic foot, the one which bears the major stress. ISP simulates this simply by making the target duration longer for these special feet.

A foot is a succession of syllables. But in living speech, the duration of the foot is not divided evenly between the syllables that make it up. Syllables have a definite rhythm of their own. In fact, music teachers often use words like "Amsterdam" to help their students remember particular musical rhythms. Syllable rhythm seems to depend upon the nature of the first syllable of the foot, and the positions of word boundaries. The first syllable tends to be long if it contains one of the so-called *long* vowels which were mentioned in Chapter 1. For example, "cut" is short, whereas "caught" is long because it contains the long vowel *aw*. A syllable will also be long even when its vowel is short, if there is more than one consonant after the vowel. "Kilt," for instance, is long, though "kit" is short. The pattern of syllables and word boundaries governs the rhythm of the foot.

Having decided how to choose foot durations, and how the syllable rhythm splits the foot duration among the individual syllables, you next have to consider how to get from syllable durations to phoneme segment durations. One important factor here is that the length of the vowel in a syllable is a strong clue to whether the final consonant is voiced. If you say in pairs words like "cap," "cab"; "cat," "cad"; "tack," "tag," you will find that the vowel in the first word of each pair is a lot shorter than that in the second. In fact, the major difference between these pairs is the vowel length, not the final consonant.

We can take this effect into account by dividing a syllable into a group of consonants at the beginning, followed by a vowel or maybe a diphthong and another group of consonants at the end. Any of these elements can be missing. The most unusual case where there is no middle occurs, for example, with the so-called *syllabic n*. This happens in words like "button" and "pudding" when they are pronounced in a way which might be written "butt'n," "pudd'n." Rules can be used to apportion the syllable duration between the initial consonants, the middle part, and the final consonants. These must distinguish between situations where the final consonants are voiced or unvoiced, to make the characteristic differences in vowel lengths.

4.3.2. Pitch

There are two basically different ways of looking at the pitch of an utterance. One is to imagine pitch *levels* attached to individual syllables. Some people have even gone so far as to associate pitch values with levels of stress, so that the more stressed a syllable is, the higher its pitch. This oversimplifies things too much, however, for we have seen that stress is associated more with change in pitch than with the pitch value itself. The second approach is to consider the variation of pitch as a graph of pitch against time, as we did earlier when looking at transferring pitch from one utterance to another. Then you need be concerned only with the overall shape of the variation rather than having to decide on the pitch for each individual syllable. However, it raises the problem of how the pitch is supposed to be fitted to the utterance. The notation just introduced helps by marking the most prominent, or "tonic," syllable with an "*."

We will look at a particular classification of pitch patterns in English which was developed by a linguist called Halliday, and is described in his book, which is listed as further reading at the end of this chapter. Halliday used the word "contour" to indicate the graph of pitch against time. Although this doesn't seem to be a very good term, I will use it too, for it's hard to find a significantly better one.

There are five different primary intonation contours, each hinging on the tonic syllable. They are sketched in Figure 4.3, which shows an imaginary conversation invented by Halliday which uses all five contours. Several secondary contours, which are variations on the primary ones, are defined as well. This classification scheme is intended for consumption by people, who have a wealth of prior knowledge of language and years of experience with it! It includes only the gross features of the infinite variety of pitch patterns found in living speech. It tries to distinguish the features which make a logical difference to the listener, and is not concerned with the acoustic details of pitch.

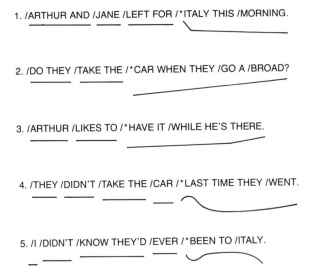

1. /ARTHUR AND /JANE /LEFT FOR /*ITALY THIS /MORNING.

2. /DO THEY /TAKE THE /*CAR WHEN THEY /GO A /BROAD?

3. /ARTHUR /LIKES TO /*HAVE IT /WHILE HE'S THERE.

4. /THEY /DIDN'T /TAKE THE /CAR /*LAST TIME THEY /WENT.

5. /I /DIDN'T /KNOW THEY'D /EVER /*BEEN TO /ITALY.

Figure 4.3 The five primary intonation contours (after Halliday, 1970).

If you want to use these contours for synthetic speech, you need first to embellish them with more detailed variation. For example, pitch is hardly ever exactly constant in living speech. So the stretches with constant pitch which precede the tonic syllable in contours 1, 2, and 3 sound most unnatural when synthesized. You need some variation in the pitch before the tonic syllable which emphasizes the natural stress on the first syllable of each foot. A "lilting" effect which reaches a peak at each foot boundary sounds quite natural. The size of the inflection can be altered slightly to add interest. If it is very large, the utterance will sound more emphatic.

The aim of the pitch assignment method of ISP is to help people to make computers talk. This means that when you enter a message to be spoken, you should have considerable control over its intonation. But you shouldn't have to be concerned with the internal details of feet or syllables. The basic notation for entering utterances was described above. However, ISP lets you define pitch contours yourself.

Each pitch contour applies to a single tone group, and is specified by ten numbers. The effect of these numbers has been chosen to give a useful range of contours. The overall pitch movement is controlled by giving the pitch at three places: the beginning of the tone group, the beginning of the tonic syllable, and the end of the tone group. You can make an abrupt pitch break at the start of the tonic syllable in order to simulate contours like 2 and 3 of Figure 4.3, and, to a lesser extent, contours 4 and 5. The points at which pitch is specified are joined by straight lines. You can also specify a dip on the tonic syllable, for emphasis, as shown in Figure 4.4.

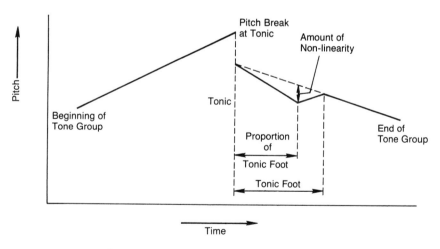

Figure 4.4 Basic shape of synthetic pitch contour.

On this basic shape are superimposed two smaller pitch patterns. The most important of these is a foot pattern which is given to each pretonic foot, so that the stressed syllables of the pretonic have added prominence and the monotony of constant pitch is avoided. This is indicated by a parameter which distorts the contour on each foot, as shown in Figure 4.5. The other is an

initialization-continuation option that allows the pitch to rise or fall independently on the initial and final feet, without affecting the contour on the rest of
the tone group (Figure 4.6).

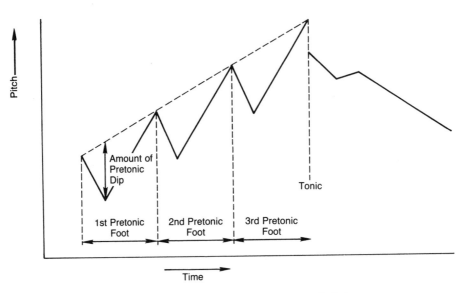

Figure 4.5 Shape of contour on pretonic feet.

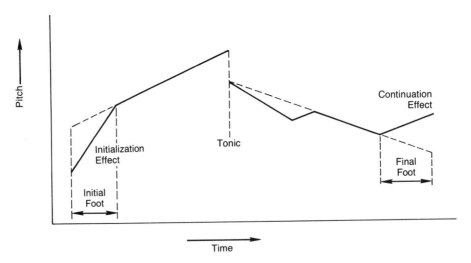

Figure 4.6 Initialization and continuation effects.

TABLE 4.1 THE QUANTITIES THAT DEFINE
A PITCH CONTOUR

A	continuation from previous tone group
	zero gives no continuation
	nonzero gives pitch at start of tone group
B	notional pitch at start
C	range on whole of pretonic
D	dip on each foot of pretonic
E	change at start of tonic
F	range on tonic
G	dip on tonic
H	continuation to next tone group
	zero gives no continuation
	nonzero gives pitch at end of tone group
I	percentage along foot of the dip, for pretonic feet
J	percentage along foot of the dip, for the tonic foot

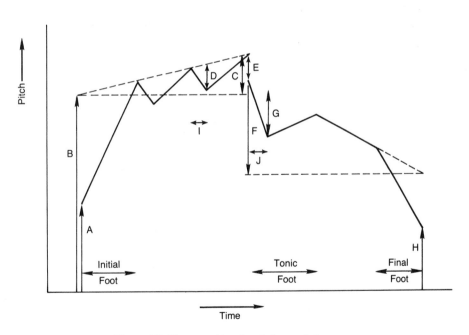

Figure 4.7 The quantities that define a pitch contour.

The ten quantities that define a pitch contour are summarized in Table 4.1, and shown diagrammatically in Figure 4.7. One basic requirement of the pitch assignment scheme was the ability to generate contours which

TABLE 4.2 PITCH CONTOUR TABLE FOR HALLIDAY'S PRIMARY TONE GROUPS

Tone group	A	B	C	D	E	F	G	H	I	J
1	0	175	0	−40	0	−100	−40	0	33%	50%
2	0	280	0	−40	−190	100	0	0	33%	50%
3	0	175	0	−40	−70	45	−10	0	33%	50%
4	0	280	−100	−40	20	45	−45	0	33%	50%
5	0	175	60	−40	−20	−45	45	0	33%	50%

approximate Halliday's five primary tone groups. Values of the ten quantities are given in Table 4.2, for each tone group. All pitches are given in Hz. A distinctly dipping pitch movement has been given to each pretonic foot, using parameter D, to lend prominence to their first syllables.

4.4. READING FROM TEXT

If you really need your computer to start with plain text, you will face some very difficult problems. The text should be understood, first of all, and then decisions have to be made about how it is to be interpreted. For an excellent speaker—like an actor—these decisions will be artistic, at least in part. They should certainly depend upon the opinion and attitude of the speaker, and how he or she feels the listener will react. Very little is known about this upper level of speech synthesis from text. In practice it is almost completely ignored—and the speech is often barely intelligible, and generally uncomfortable to listen to. If you are thinking of building or using a speech output system which starts from something close to plain text, you should consider carefully whether some extra information can be coded into the initial input to help the computer. Usually you can do this. However, reading machines for the blind are a good example of a situation where arbitrary, unannotated texts must be read.

4.4.1. Intonation   One distinction which a program can usefully try to make is between basically rising and basically falling pitch contours. People often say that pitch rises on a question and falls on a statement, but if you listen to speech, you will find that this is a gross oversimplification. It normally falls on complete statements, certainly, but it falls as often as it rises on questions. It is more accurate to say that pitch rises on "yes-no" questions and falls on other utterances, although this is still only a rough guide. A simple rule is to determine whether a sentence is a question by looking at the punctuation mark at its end, and then to examine the first word. If it is a "wh"-word like "what," "which," "when," "why" (and also "how"), a falling contour is likely to fit. If not, the question is probably a yes-no one, and the contour should rise. Such a crude rule will certainly not be very accurate. It fails, for example, when the "wh"-word is embedded in a phrase as in "at what time are you going?" But at least it provides a starting point.

You give an air of finality to an utterance when you say it with a definite fall in pitch, and drop to a rather low value at the end. This should accompany the last intonation unit in an utterance, unless it's a yes-no question. However, a rise-fall pattern such as contour 5 in Figure 4.3 can easily be used in utterance-final position by one person in a conversation—although it would be unlikely to terminate the dialogue altogether. A new topic is frequently introduced by a fall-rise intonation—such as contour 4 of Figure 4.3—and this often begins a paragraph.

Determining the type of pitch contour is only one part of intonation. There are really three separate problems: dividing the utterance into tone groups, choosing the tonic syllable or major stress point of each one, and assigning a pitch contour to each tone group. Let's continue to use Halliday's notation for intonation. Moreover, assume for now that the foot boundaries can be placed correctly. Then a scheme which uses only the printed form of the utterance and does not attempt to "understand" it is as follows:

- Place a tone group boundary at every punctuation mark

- Place the tonic at the first syllable of the last foot in a tone group

- Use contour 4 for the first tone group in a paragraph

- Use contour 2 for a yes-no question

- Use contour 1 elsewhere.

These extremely crude and simplistic rules are really about all you can do without trying to make a complicated analysis of what the text means. They actually seem to do the right thing a surprising amount of the time. Table 4.3 shows part of a spontaneous monologue which was transcribed by Halliday and appears in his teaching text on intonation. There are some prosodic symbols that we have not seen before. First, each of the five contours in Figure 4.3 has variants which are identified by "1 + ", "1 − " for contour 1, and so on. Second, the mark "..." is used to indicate a pause which disrupts the speech rhythm. Third, compound tone groups such as "13" appear which contain *two* tonic syllables. These are not the same as what you get by simply following one contour by the other, like contour 1 followed by contour 3 in this case, because the first in some sense dominates the second. Typically the first clause gives the main information, while the second forms an adjunct clause.

Applying the simple rules given above to the text of Table 4.3 leads to the results of Table 4.4. Three-quarters of the tone group boundaries are flagged by punctuation marks, with no extra ones being included. Eighty-eight percent of tone groups have a tonic syllable at the start of the final foot. However, the compound tone groups each have two tonic syllables, and of course only the second one is predicted by the final-foot rule. Assigning intonation contours on

TABLE 4.3 EXAMPLE OF INTONATION AND RHYTHM ANALYSIS

Plain text	Text adorned with prosodic markers
From Scarborough to Whitby is a	4 ˆ from /Scarborough to /*Whitby is a
very pleasant journey, with	1 — very /pleasant /*journey with
very beautiful countryside.	1 — very /beautiful /*countryside ...
In fact the Yorkshire coast is	1 + ˆ in /fact the /Yorkshire /coast is
lovely,	/*lovely
all along, ex-	1 + all a/*long ex
cept the parts that are covered	— 4 cept the /parts that are /covered
in caravans of course; and	in /*caravans of /course and
if you go in spring,	4 if you /go in /*spring
when the gorse is out,	4 ˆ when the /*gorse is /out
or in summer,	4 ˆ or in /*summer
when the heather's out,	4 ˆ when the /*heather's /out
it's really one of the most	13 ˆ it's /really /one of the /most
delightful areas in the	de/*lightful /*areas in the
whole country.	1 whole /*country
The moorland is	4 ˆ the /*moorland is
rather high up, and	1 rather /high /*up and
fairly flat — a	1 fairly /*flat a
sort of plateau.	1 sort of /*plateau ...
At least,	1 ˆ at /*least
it isn't really flat,	13 ˆ it /*isn't /really /*flat
when you get up on the top;	— 3 ˆ when you /get up on the /*top
it's rolling moorland	1 ˆ it's /rolling /*moorland
cut across by steep valleys. But	1 cut across by /steep /*valleys but
seen from the coast it's	4 seen from the /*coast it's ...
"up there on the moors", and you	1 up there on the /*moors and you
always think of it as a	— 4 always /*think of it as a
kind of tableland.	1 kind of /*tableland

the extremely simple basis of using contour 4 for the first tone group in a paragraph, and contour 1 thereafter, also seems to work quite well. Variant contours such as "1 +" and "1 —" have been treated as though they were the appropriate primary contour (1, in this case) for the present purpose, and compound tone groups have been assigned the first contour of the pair. The result is that 68 percent of contours are given correctly.

These results are really astonishingly good, considering the crudeness of the rules. However, they should be interpreted with caution. What is missed by the rules, although appearing to comprise only 20 to 30 percent of the features, is certain to include the important, information-bearing, and variety-producing features that make the utterance alive and interesting. It would be rash to assume that all tone-group boundaries, all tonic positions, and all intonation contours are equally important for intelligibility and naturalness. It is much more likely that the rules predict a default pattern, while most

TABLE 4.4 SUCCESS OF SIMPLE INTONATION ASSIGNMENT RULES

Number of tone groups	25
Number of boundaries correctly placed	19 (76%)
Number of boundaries incorrectly placed	0
Number of tone groups having a tonic syllable at the beginning of the final foot	22 (88%)
Number of tone groups whose contours are correctly assigned	17 (68%)
Number of compound tone groups	2 (8%)
Number of variant contours	7 (28%)

information is borne by deviations from them. Certainly if you synthesize the utterance with intonation given by these rules, it will sound extremely dull and repetitive. This is mainly because of the overwhelming predominance of tone group 1 and the fact that tonic stress is always placed on the final foot.

There are certainly many different ways to speak any particular text, and that reproduced in Table 4.3 is only one possible version. However, it is fair to say that the default intonation discussed above could occur naturally only under very unusual circumstances. It is like a petulant child, unwilling and sulky, having been forced to read aloud. This is hardly how we want our computers to speak.

4.4.2. Rhythm   How are we going to decide where to place foot boundaries in English text? Certainly the meaning sometimes plays a part in this. You could say

/⌃ is /this /train /going /*to /London

instead of the more usual

/⌃ is /this /train /going to /*London

in circumstances where the train might be going *to* or *from* London. We will have to ignore such complications, although it is worth noting in passing that the rogue words will often be marked by an underline or italics—as in the previous sentence. If the text is liberally underlined, you probably won't need to analyze the meaning for the purposes of rhythm.

A rough and ready rule for placing foot boundaries is to insert one before each word which is not in a small closed set of "function words." These include, for example, "a," "and," "but," "for," "is," "the," "to." If a verb or adjective begins with a prefix, the boundary should be moved between it and the root—but not for a noun. This will make the distinction between the *con*vert and to con*vert*, the *ex*tract and to ex*tract*, and for many North

American speakers will help to distinguish *in*quiry from in*quire*. However, detecting prefixes by a simple splitting algorithm is dangerous. For example, "predate" is a verb with stress on what appears to be a prefix, contrary to the rule. The "pre" in "predator" is not a prefix—at least, it is not pronounced as the prefix "pre" normally is. Polysyllabic words like "*dip*lomat," "dip*lo*macy," "diplo*ma*tic"; or "*tel*egraph," "te*le*graphy," "tele*graph*ic," cannot be handled on such a simple basis.

4.4.3. Speech Synthesis from Concept   We have seen that in order to derive prosodic features of an utterance from text, you need to understand its role in the dialogue, its meaning, its part of speech, and the structure of its prefixes. This is a very tall order. The problem of natural language comprehension by machine is a vast research area in its own right. However, in many circumstances when you want to make computers talk, utterances are generated from internally stored data rather than by being read aloud from preprepared text. Then the problem of understanding text input may be evaded, for presumably the language-generation program can provide some information about the meaning and part of speech of the words. It should also be able to indicate the role of each utterance in the dialogue, because it must know why it is necessary to say it.

This forms the basis of the appealing notion of "speech synthesis from concept." It has some advantages over speech generation from text, and in principle should provide a more natural-sounding result. Every word produced by the system can have a complete dictionary entry which shows its prefixes and potential stress points. A full grammatical parsing of each utterance is known.

However, it is not clear how to take advantage of any information about meaning which is available. Ideally, the computer should be possible to place tone group boundaries and tonic stress points, and decide on intonation contours, all in a natural-sounding way. But look again at the example text of Table 4.3 and imagine that you have at your disposal as much semantic information as is needed. It is *still* far from obvious how to decide on the intonation features. In the ultimate analysis, it is interpretive and stylistic *choices* that add variety and interest to speech.

Take the problem of determining pitch contours, for instance. You might be able to explain some of them. Contour 4 on

> except the parts that are covered in caravans of course

is due to its being a contrastive clause, for it presents essentially new information. Similarly, the succession

> if you go in spring
> when the gorse is out
> or in summer
> when the heather's out

could be considered contrastive, because it is an "if" clause and therefore contrasts with the unspoken "if not." So this could explain why contour 4s were used. But this is all conjecture, and it is difficult to apply throughout the passage. It is possible to explain the contexts in which each tone group is typically used, but only in an extremely high-level manner which would be impossible to implement directly in a computer program. Computer systems for generating written English do not provide the subtle information needed to make decisions about intonation.

As another example, look at the passage given at the top of Table 4.5. Before looking at the comments on selected words in the body of the table, you should read the passage aloud two or three times. The comments are selected and slightly edited from those appearing in a PhD thesis written in 1968 by Ralph Vanderslice at Los Angeles. He called his thesis "synthetic elocution," and looked hard at the deep problems of why people choose to say things the way they do.

TABLE 4.5 SAMPLE PASSAGE AND COMMENTS FOR SYNTHETIC ELOCUTION

Human experience and human behavior are accessible to observation by everyone. The psychologist tries to bring them under systematic study. What he perceives, however, anyone can perceive; for his task he requires no microscope or electronic gear.

	Word	Comments
1	Human	special treatment because paragraph-initial
4	human	accent deleted because it echoes word 1
13	psychologist	emphasis assigned because of antithesis with "everyone"
17	them	anaphoric to "Human experience and human behavior"
19	systematic	emphasis assigned because of contrast with "observation"
20	study	emphasis? — text is ambiguous whether "observation" is a kind of study that is nonsystematic, or an activity contrasting with the entire concept of "systematic study"
21	What	increase in pitch for "What he perceives" because it is not the subject
22	he	accented although anaphoric to word 13 because of antithesis with word 25
24	however	decrease in pitch because it is parenthetical
25	anyone	emphasized by antithesis with word 22
27	perceive	unaccented because it echoes word 23, "perceives"
	;	semicolon assigns falling intonation
30	task	unaccented because it is anaphoric with "tries to bring them under systematic study"

Now look at the comments on individual words. The words are numbered to help you find them in the passage. Some of the comments mention "accent" and "emphasis"; these relate to stress. Roughly speaking, "accent" encompasses both foot-initial stress and tonic stress, whereas "emphasis" is something more than this. You get emphasis by using the fall-rise or rise-fall contours, shown as contours 4 and 5 of Figure 4.3.

A lot of attention is paid to the concepts of anaphora and antithesis. The first term means the repetition of a word or phrase in the text, and is often applied to pronouns. In the example, the word "human" is repeated in the first phrase. "Them" in the second sentence refers to "human experience and human behavior." "He" in the third sentence is the previously mentioned psychologist. These are all anaphoric references. A more complicated one is "task," which is anaphoric with "tries to bring them under systematic study." Other things being equal, anaphoric references are not accented, because they don't introduce new ideas or new names. In terms of our intonation contours, this means that they certainly don't receive tonic stress and may not even get foot stress.

Antithesis is defined as the contrast of ideas expressed by parallelism of strongly contrasting words or phrases. The second element taking part in it is generally emphasized, by using fall-rise or rise-fall contours. "Psychologist" in the passage is an antithesis of "everyone." "Systematic" is an antithesis of "observation." Thus

/‸ the psy/*chologist

would probably receive intonation contour 4, since it is also introducing a new actor. On the other hand,

/tries to /bring them /under /system/*matic /study

involves antithesis but not a new actor, so it could receive contour 5. "He" (word 22) is anaphorical as well as antithetical. Because it is anaphorical with "psychologist," it should have its accent removed. However, it is antithetical with "everyone"—for the passage is bringing out a contrast between the way in which psychologists perceive things and the way in which everyone else does. Hence its accent, which would have been removed, is restored again. It will certainly begin a foot, and possibly a tonic foot.

Anaphora and antithesis provide an ideal domain for speech synthesis from concept, rather than from text. Determining them from plain English text is a very difficult problem, requiring a great deal of real-world knowledge. Automatic detection of anaphora has been looked at by people concerned with natural language understanding. Surprisingly, perhaps, finding pronoun referents is an important problem for language translation. Suppose you were translating sentences such as

I bought the wine, sat on a table, and drank it
I bought the wine, sat on a table, and broke it

into French. The "it" refers to different things in each case, the wine in the first sentence and the table in the second. This is important to know, because in French, "wine" and "table" have different genders—it is *le* vin, but *la* table.

In spoken language, emphasis is used to indicate the referent of a pronoun when it would not otherwise be obvious. In the examples

Bill saw John across the room and he ran over to him
Bill saw John across the room and *he* ran over to *him*

the emphasis reverses the pronoun referents so that John did the running. In speech, you accent a personal pronoun whenever the true antecedent is not the same as the one that people would otherwise assume. Unfortunately, it is difficult to decide what it is that people would otherwise assume. Does it mean that the referent cannot be predicted from knowledge of the words alone—as in the second example above? If so, this is a clear candidate for speech synthesis from concept, for it is *impossible* to make the distinction from text!

4.5. PRONUNCIATION

We have talked about getting prosodic information about the way things should be said from plain text. How about the phonetic information? We need to be able to write computer programs which can "pronounce" English, that is, look at a written word and translate it into phonetic form.

Everyone knows that English pronunciation is very irregular. Ask anyone who has learned it as a foreign language! You might think that the only thing we can do is to store a complete pronunciation dictionary. But remember the discussion at the beginning of the last chapter about how there really are a lot of different words, if you count inflected forms as different (like "words," "wordy," "wording," "wordings," "worded," "wordiness," "word-painting," "word-perfect," "word-picture," "word-play," "word-splitting"). Surely we can do better than storing *everything* in a pronunciation dictionary.

Actually, despite the irregularity, it is surprising how much can be done with simple letter-to-sound rules. These specify the pronunciation of word fragments and single letters. The longest stored fragment which matches the current word is translated, and then the same strategy is repeated on the remainder of the word. Table 4.6 shows some English fragments and their pronunciations.

It is sometimes important that a rule applies only when the fragment is matched at the beginning or end of a word. In the table, "-" means that other fragments can precede or follow this one. The "|" sign is used to separate suffixes from a word stem, as will be explained shortly.

An advantage of choosing the longest matching fragment that can be found in the dictionary is that it is easy to account for exceptions simply by putting them into the fragment table. Suppose you put a complete word, whose pronunciation does not obey the rules, into the fragment table. If it occurs in the input, the whole word will automatically be matched first, before any fragment of it is translated. The exception list of complete words can be surprisingly small for quite respectable performance.

TABLE 4.6 WORD
FRAGMENTS AND THEIR
PRONUNCIATIONS

Fragment	Pronunciation
-p-	*p*
-ph-	*f*
-phe|	*f ee*
-phe|s	*f ee z*
-phot-	*f uh u t*
-place|-	*p l e i s*
-plac|i-	*p l e i s i*
-ple|ment-	*p l i m e n t*
-plie|-	*p l aa i y*
-post	*p uh u s t*
-pp-	*p*
-pp|ly-	*p l ee*
-preciou-	*p r e s uh*
-proce|d-	*p r uh u s ee d*
-prope|r-	*p r o p uh r*
-prov-	*p r uu v*
-purpose-	*p er p uh s*
-push-	*p u sh*
-put	*p u t*
-puts	*p u t s*

Table 4.7 shows the entire dictionary for an excellent early pronunciation system written at Bell Laboratories in 1974. Some of the words are notorious exceptions in English, while others are included simply because the rules would run amok on them. The exceptions are all quite short—only a few of them have more than two syllables.

Special action has to be taken with final "e"s. These lengthen and alter the quality of the preceding vowel, so that "bit" becomes "bite" and so on. Unfortunately, if the word has a suffix, the "e" must be detected even though it is no longer final, as in "lonely," and it is even dropped sometimes, as in "biting"—otherwise these would be pronounced "lonelly," "bitting." To make matters worse, the suffix may be another word—we don't want "kiteflying" to have an extra syllable after the "kit" which rhymes with "*tef*lon"!

Simple procedures can be developed to take care of common word endings like "-ly" "-ness" "-d." Compound words are more difficult. Look at "wisecrack" and "bumblebee." You have to be able to decompose them into "wise-crack" and "bumble-bee"; otherwise you would pronounce them with three syllables instead of two. To decompose them, you really have to know that "wise," "crack," "bumble," and "bee" are all words in their own right. This needs a large dictionary.

TABLE 4.7 EXCEPTION TABLE FOR A SIMPLE PRONUNCIATION
PROGRAM

a	doesn't	guest	meant	reader	those
alkali	doing	has	moreover	refer	to
always	done	have	mr	says	today
any	dr	having	mrs	seven	tomorrow
april	early	heard	nature	shall	Tuesday
are	earn	his	none	someone	two
as	eleven	imply	nothing	something	upon
because	enable	into	nowhere	than	very
been	engine	is	nuisance	that	water
being	etc	island	of	the	Wednesday
below	evening	John	on	their	were
body	every	July	once	them	who
both	everyone	live	one	there	whom
busy	February	lived	only	thereby	whose
copy	finally	living	over	these	woman
do	Friday	many	people	they	women
does	gas	maybe	read	this	yes

There are, of course, exceptions to the final "e" rule. Many common
words like "some," "done," and the verb "to live," disobey the rule by not
lengthening the main vowel.   In other, rarer cases like "anemone,"
"catastrophe," and "epitome" the final "e" is actually pronounced. There are
also some complete anomalies like "fete."

Here is a procedure, taken from the Bell Laboratories system mentioned
earlier, that pronounces English words using these ideas. It is a superb example
of a robust program which takes a pragmatic approach to the problems.
Accepting that they will never be fully solved, it behaves as gracefully as possible when it gets out of its depth. The pronunciation of each word is found by
a succession of increasingly desperate trials:

- Replace upper- by lowercase letters, strip punctuation, and try again.

- Remove final "s," replace final "ie" by "y," and try again.

- Reject a word without a vowel.

- Repeatedly mark any suffixes with "|."

- Mark with "|" probable divisions in compound words.

- Mark potential long vowels indicated by "e|," and long vowels elsewhere
  in the word.

- Mark voiced medial "s" as in "busy," "usual"; replace final "-s" if
  stripped.

- Scanning the word from left to right, apply letter-to-sound rules to word fragments.

- When all else fails, spell the word, punctuation and all.

- Burp on letters for which no spelling rule exists.

Table 4.8 shows the suffixes which the program recognizes. Multiple suffixes are detected and marked in words like "force|ful|ly" and "spite|ful|ness." This allows silent "e"s to be spotted even when they occur far back in a word. The suffix marks are available to the word-fragment rules of Table 4.6, and they are often used.

TABLE 4.8 RULES FOR
DETECTING SUFFIXES FOR
FINAL 'E' PROCESSING

Suffix	Action
s	strip off final s
'	strip off final '
ie	replace final ie by y
| able	place suffix mark as shown
| ably	
e | d	
e | n	
e | r	
e | ry	
e | st	
e | y	
| ful	
| ing	
| less	
| ly	
| ment	
| ness	
| or	
| ic	place suffix mark as shown
| ical	and terminate final 'e'
e |	processing

The program has some *ad hoc* rules for dealing with compound words like "race|track," "house|boat." These are applied as well as normal suffix splitting so that multiple decompositions like "pace|make|r" can be accomplished. The rules look for short letter sequences which usually only appear in compound words. But it is impossible to detect every compound-word boundary like this, and the program inevitably makes mistakes. For example, the boundaries in "edge|ways," "fence|post," "horse|back," "large|mouth," and "where|in" go undetected. Boundaries are incorrectly inserted into "comple|mentary," "male|volent," "prole|tariat," "Pame|la."

I rewrote this program myself for my laboratory computer a few years ago, on the basis of a published Bell Laboratories description of it. It first worked one Friday, just before lunch, and as we were about to go for some refreshment the first thing I made it say was "a pint of Guinness." The result was rather surprising. "Pint" came out rhyming with "mint." Actually, when you think about it, it is rather an unusual word, for it doesn't rhyme with "tint," "hint," or "lint." It's just a plain exception. "Guinness" came out like "gwyniss," on the basis that "gui" is pronounced as in "penguin" and "anguish." In this case the rule was applied even at the beginning of a word, which it should not be because "guitar" and "guilt" have a hard "g" too. This was quickly fixed.

The program makes do with a tiny exception dictionary, even though we know that English has an enormous number of unusual pronunciations. However, many of the unusual pronunciations are for relatively uncommon words. The program has been tested against the 2000 most frequent words of English. If you take word frequencies into account, 97 percent of them are pronounced correctly. This means that there is a 97 percent chance that a random word chosen from a newspaper (say) will be pronounced properly. However, success will be much less likely on a random word taken from a dictionary or word list, because an uncommon word like "pint" is just as likely as a common one like "but."

4.6. DISCUSSION

This chapter has really only touched the tip of a linguistic iceberg. I have given some examples of representations, rules, algorithms, and exceptions, to make the concepts more tangible, but a whole mass of detail has been swept under the carpet.

There are two important messages that are worth repeating again. The first is that the representation of the input is crucial to the quality of the output. The input might be a "concept" in some semantic notation, a grammatical breakdown of the parts of speech in an utterance, a decomposition into suffixes and prefixes, plain text or some contrived respelling of it. Almost any extra information can be taken into account and used to improve the speech. It is very difficult to obtain this information if it isn't provided explicitly.

Second, simple algorithms perform remarkably well. For example, we looked at a punctuation-driven scheme for deciding on intonation, and simple word-fragment rules for pronunciation. But the apparent success of these procedures should be interpreted with care. Information theory, and common sense, tell us that the more unusual a word, the more information it carries.

Similarly, the less predictable an intonation pattern, the more information it conveys. Although our simple rules may not fail often, they fail at the most important places. Also, when several imperfect processes are all used in producing speech, the result will be quite bad. Each process contributes its bit to the poor quality, and great complexity will be introduced if you want to discard these simple algorithms and use more sophisticated ones. There is, for instance, a world of difference between a pronunciation program that copes with 97 percent of common words and one that deals correctly with 99 percent of a random sample from a dictionary.

Some of the representations that can be used in a speech synthesis system are summarized in Figure 4.8. Starting from text, you can take the simple approach of stripping off suffixes on the basis of letter patterns, use letter-to-sound rules for pronunciation, and derive intonation from punctuation. This will all be fairly easy to implement, but the speech quality will probably not be acceptable to any but the most dedicated listener (such as a blind person with no other access to reading material).

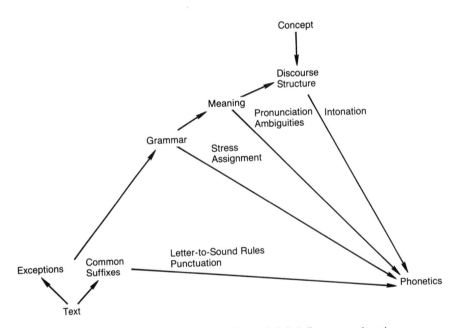

Figure 4.8 Levels in text understanding and their influence on elocution.

You would get a vast improvement in speech quality by providing more intelligent control over intonation. This, unfortunately, is awfully difficult to do—unless intonation contours, tonic stresses, and tone-group boundaries are marked by hand in the input. To generate the appropriate information from text one has to climb to the upper levels in Figure 4.8—and even when these are reached, the problems are by no means over. Still, let us climb the tree.

For grammatical analysis, you need information about parts of speech. For this you must ascertain the grammatical roles of individual words. You will need a large dictionary. Now that you have the grammatical structure, you can apply rules to produce more natural speech rhythms. You will also be able to make improvements to the pronunciation, particularly in the case of silent "e"s in compound words. But your ability to decide on appropriate intonation has hardly been improved at all.

Onward and upward. Now the problems become really difficult. You need a semantic representation of the text, but what exactly does this mean? You will need to resolve pronoun references to help assign stress. Parts of the problem are solved in principle by people working on artificial intelligence, but if you want to incorporate this into your speech synthesis system it will become enormously complicated. In addition, we have seen that you need to know about antitheses in the text. Procedures for extracting this information constitute a major research project.

Now step back and look at things from a broader point of view. What could we do with this semantic understanding and knowledge of the structure of the discourse if we had it? Suppose the input were a "concept" in some as yet undetermined representation. What are the *acoustic* manifestations of such high-level features as anaphoric references or antithetical comparisons, of parenthetical or satirical remarks, of emotions: warmth, sarcasm, sadness, and despair? Can we program the art of elocution? These are good questions.

4.7. FURTHER READING

Abercrombie, D., *Studies in Phonetics and Linguistics*. London, England: Oxford University Press, 1965. Abercrombie is one of the leading English authorities on phonetics, and this is a collection of essays which he has written over the years. Some of them treat prosodics explicitly, and others show the influence of verse structure on Abercrombie's thinking.

Bolinger, D., ed., *Intonation*. Middlesex, England: Penguin, 1972. A collection of papers that treat a wide variety of different aspects of intonation in living speech.

Crystal, D., *Prosodic Systems and Intonation in English*. Cambridge, England: Cambridge University Press, 1969. This book attempts to develop a theoretical basis for the study of British English intonation.

Halliday, M.A.K., *A Course in Spoken English: Intonation*. London, England: Oxford University Press, 1970. This book, intended for teaching foreign students about English intonation, introduces and describes the classification of intonation contours that has been used in this chapter. There are many illustrations, examples, and exercises. This makes the book accessible even to those who are not interested in the finer points of linguistics and phonetics.

Lehiste, I., *Suprasegmentals*. Cambridge, Massachusetts: MIT Press, 1970. Here is a comprehensive study of prosodics in natural language. It is divided into three major sections: quantity (timing), tonal features (pitch), and stress.

5

The Application Level: Interaction and Systems

Interactive computers are being used more and more by nonspecialist people without much previous computer experience. As processing costs continue to decline, the overall expense of providing highly interactive systems becomes increasingly dominated by terminal and communications equipment. Taken together, these two factors highlight the need for easy-to-use, low-bandwidth interactive terminals that make maximum use of the existing telephone network for remote access.

Speech output can provide versatile feedback from a computer at very low cost in distribution and terminal equipment. It is attractive from several points of view. Terminals—telephones—are invariably in place already. People without experience of computers are accustomed to their use, and are not intimidated by them. The telephone network is cheap to use and extends all over the world. The touchtone keypad, or a portable tone generator, provides a complementary data input device which will do for many purposes until the technology of speech recognition becomes better developed and more widespread. Indeed, many applications—especially information retrieval ones—need much less communication from user to computer than in the reverse direction, and voice output combined with restricted keypad entry provides a good match to their requirements.

There are, however, formidable problems in implementing natural and useful interactive systems using speech output. The eye can absorb information at a far greater rate than can the ear. You can scan a page of text in a way which has no analogy in auditory terms. Even so, it is difficult to design an interface which allows you to search computer output visually at high speed. In practice, scanning a new report is often better done at your desk with a printed copy than at a computer terminal with a viewing program—although this is likely to change in the near future.

With speech, the problem of organizing output becomes even harder. It's like looking through a tiny window which is hard to move around. Imagine reading a newspaper through a keyhole! Most of the information we learn using our ears is presented in a conversational way, either in face-to-face discussions or over the telephone. Verbal but nonconversational presentations, as in the university lecture theater, are known to be a rather inefficient way of transmitting information. In fact, the most you can do in a lecture is to communicate enthusiasm, motivation, and opinion rather than facts. The degree of interaction is extremely high even in a telephone conversation. Communication relies heavily on speech gestures, such as hesitations, grunts, and pauses; on prosodic features, such as intonation, pitch range, tempo, and voice quality; and on conversational gambits, such as interruption and long silence.

There is also a very special problem with voice output, namely, the transient nature of the speech signal. If you miss an utterance, it's gone. With a television terminal, at least the last few interactions usually remain available. Even then, you often look up beyond the top of the screen and wish that more of the history was still visible. This obviously places a premium on a voice response system's ability to repeat utterances. Moreover, you must do your utmost to ensure that users are always aware of where they are in the interaction, for they have no opportunity to refresh their memory by glancing at earlier entries and responses.

There are two separate aspects to the human-computer interface in a voice response system. The first is the relationship between the system and the end user, that is, the "consumer" of the synthesized dialogue. The second is the relationship between the system and the person who creates the dialogue. These are both treated in the next section. We will have more to say about the first aspect, for it is ultimately more important to more people. But facilities for creating the dialogue are important, too, for without them no systems would exist. The technical difficulty of creating synthetic dialogues for the majority of voice systems probably explains why speech output technology is still greatly underused. Then we look at techniques for using small keypads such as those on touchtone telephones, for they are an essential part of many voice response systems.

The remainder of the chapter describes some example systems which use speech output. We will look briefly at half a dozen examples, ranging from very simple ones like talking calculators to a complete reading machine for the blind. There is not space to do more than sketch the operation of these systems, and in some cases the details are clouded by commercial secrecy, which would prevent a complete description anyway. But they all rest on principles which we have studied earlier in this book.

5.1. PROGRAMMING PRINCIPLES FOR FRIENDLY TALKING COMPUTERS

You have to pay special attention to the details of the man-machine interface in speech-output systems. Most of the principles below stem from the fact that speech is both more intrusive and more ephemeral than writing. They have been distilled out of practical experience with speech systems, and are based upon observation and speculation rather than empirical research. There is an urgent need for proper studies of user psychology in speech interaction.

5.1.1. Echoing and Prompting
When you type a character on a television terminal connected to a computer, that character is "echoed" back on to the screen so that you can see what you've typed. However, repeating character by character what is typed is quite distracting and annoying if speech is the computer output medium. If you type "123" and the computer echoes

"one ... two ... three"

after the individual key-presses, it is liable to divert your attention. Voice output is much more intrusive than a purely visual "echo." It forces itself on you, rather than simply appearing on a screen for you to look at if you want.

However, you do need some confirmation of your keyboard entries; otherwise an error could be disastrous. An immediate response to a completed line of input is better than character-by-character echo. This response can take the form of a reply to a query, provided that the kind of reply makes it clear what the query was. If successive data items are being typed, the data must be confirmed somehow. It is best if the information can be spoken in the same way that you yourself would be likely to verbalize it. For example, when entering numbers:

USER: "123 # " (# is the end-of-line character)

COMPUTER: "One hundred twenty-three."

You may be able to use intonation to advantage here, with an incomplete, rising pitch for intermediate entries and a final, falling one for the last entry. If the query requires lengthy processing, the input should be summarized in a neat, meaningful form to give the user a chance to abort the request.

The computer will have to prompt the user for each entry by saying things like "enter next number." Such prompts are, of course, used in nonspeech-based systems as well. Computer-generated prompts must be explicit and frequent enough to allow new users to understand what they are expected to do. Experienced users will "type ahead" quite naturally, entering the data before the prompt is completed or even before it has begun. It is most helpful if the computer suppresses unnecessary prompts when this happens. It can easily do this by inspecting the input buffer before prompting. Then, experienced users who can anticipate what they have to type next can just go ahead without waiting. In this way they can join together frequently used sequences of commands into mental chunks which are thought of as a single sequence. The size of these chunks is entirely at the user's own discretion. This provides a very natural way for the system to adapt itself automatically to the experience of the user. New users will naturally wait to be prompted, and will proceed through the dialogue at a slower and more relaxed pace.

Suppressing unnecessary prompts is a good idea in any interactive system, whether or not it uses the medium of speech—although it is hardly ever done in conventional systems. It is particularly important with speech, however, because an unexpected or unwanted prompt is quite distracting, and it is not so easy to ignore as it is with a visual display. Furthermore, speech messages take longer to present than displayed ones, so that the user is distracted for more time.

Another issue is what the system should do if it is expecting input and none arrives for a significant time. Should it "time out" and repeat the prompt after a while? In general, input timeouts are dangerous, because they may give the user the feeling of not being in control of the computer system. For example, a case has been reported where a user became highly agitated and refused to go near the terminal again after his first timed-out prompt. He had been quietly thinking what to do and the terminal suddenly interjecting and making its own suggestions was just too much for him. However, voice response systems lack the satisfying visual feedback that ending a line gives on a television terminal or printer. It seems that a timed-out reminder may be appropriate if there is a delay after some characters have been entered.

5.1.2. Giving Information

Lengthy computer voice responses are not effective at conveying information. Attention wanders if you are not actively involved in the conversation. A sequential exchange of terse messages, each designed to dispense one small unit of information, forces the user to take a meaningful part in the dialogue. It has other advantages, too, allowing a higher degree of input-dependent branching, and permitting rapid recovery from errors.

The following example from an audio response system designed to help physicians to diagnose acidosis, is a good example of what *not* to do.

> "(Chime) A VALUE OF SIX-POINT-ZERO-ZERO HAS BEEN ENTERED FOR PH. THIS VALUE IS IMPOSSIBLE. TO CONTINUE THE PROGRAM, ENTER A NEW VALUE FOR PH IN THE RANGE BETWEEN SIX-POINT-SIX AND EIGHT-POINT-ZERO (beep dah beep-beep)."

The system uses extraneous noises like a "chime" to herald an error message, and a "beep dah beep-beep" to request data input in the form <digit> <point> <digit> <digit>. This was thought necessary by the designers to keep users awake and help them with the format of the interaction. But rather than a long monologue like this, it seems much better to design a sequential interchange of terse messages, so that the caller can be guided into a state where an error can easily be corrected. For example,

CALLER:	"6*00#"
COMPUTER:	"Entry out of range"
CALLER:	"6*00#" (persists)
COMPUTER:	"The minimum acceptable pH value is 6.6"
CALLER:	"9*03#"
COMPUTER:	"The maximum acceptable pH value is 8.0"

This allows a quick recovery in the likely event that the entry has simply been mistyped. If the error persists, the caller is given just one piece of information at a time, and forced to continue to play an active role in the interaction.

Another factor that you should bear in mind when designing a speech dialogue is the order in which information is presented. Many menu-selection systems which use television terminals show items in an order which is inappropriate for speech. A good example is a list of items preceded by selection numbers, as used in many videotex systems:

1 — National
2 — International
3 — Business
4 — Finance
5 — . . .

The user is supposed to press the appropriate key to get the information he requires. For speech, however, it is better to give the user's action *after* the information rather than before it:

National — press one
International — press two
Business — press three
Finance — press four . . .

Although this looks a lot more messy on the printed page or television screen, it gives users the opportunity to listen for the information they require and then concentrate on how to get it, rather than the other way around. Such attention to detail is the hallmark of good interactive systems. When you design the dialogue, you should put yourself in the place of the user. Don't forget that he or she is listening, and not seeing.

A serious problem when giving information in a voice response system is that synthetic speech is usually rather dreary to listen to. You should carefully avoid successive utterances with identical intonations. Small changes in speaking rate, pitch range, and mean pitch level all help to add variety. Unfortunately, little is known at present about the part that intonation plays in human interactive dialogue. However, even random variations in the pitch are useful to relieve the tedium of repetitive intonation patterns.

5.1.3. User Actions If commands can be entered directly without explicit confirmation before they are acted upon, as I suggested above, it must always be easy for the user to revoke an action. You need an "undo" command. The usefulness of this is now commonly recognized for any interactive system, and it becomes even more important in speech systems, because it is easier for the user to make errors by losing the place in the dialogue.

A command which interrupts output and returns to a known state should be recognized at every level of the system. It is essential that voice output be terminated immediately, rather than at the end of the utterance. We do not want the user to live in fear of the system's embarking on a long, boring monologue that is impossible to interrupt. The same is true of interactive dialogues which do not use speech, but it becomes particularly important with voice response because it takes longer to present information.

Any voice response system must include a universal "repeat last utterance" command, because old output does not remain visible. A fairly sophisticated facility is desirable, as repeat requests are very frequent in practice. There are different reasons why you might want a message repeated. You might simply have been unable to understand it. Or you might have forgotten what was said. Or your attention may have been distracted—a common occurrence in an office or home environment.

These different reasons point out the need for different kinds of repeat requests. First, you must be able to have the last message repeated in case of misrecognition. It is essential not to simply regenerate another identical copy of the utterance. Some variation of intonation and rhythm is needed to prevent an annoying, stereotyped response. A second consecutive repeat request should trigger a paraphrased reply. An error recovery sequence could be used which presents the misunderstood information in a different way with more interaction, but this is probably less important if information units are kept small anyway.

If your attention has been distracted, you need to be able to get a summary of the current state of the interaction to remind you where you left off. For this, the system will have to maintain a model of the state of the user. Even a poor model, like a record of the last few transactions and their results, is well worth having.

5.1.4. What about the Programmer? The issues that we have looked at so far are ones which should be borne in mind by the computer programmer who is constructing an interactive system and designing the dialogue. But what kind of environment will provide most assistance with this work?

The best help the designer can have is a speech generation method which makes it easy to enter new utterances and modify them on line. It will be necessary to change the dialogue in cut-and-try attempts to render it as natural as possible. It's very hard to imagine what a dialogue will "feel" like without trying it out—and the designer should be encouraged to try as many alternatives as possible. This is perhaps the most important advantage of synthesizing speech by rule from text or phonetics. If recorded natural utterances are stored, it becomes quite difficult to make minor modifications to the dialogue in the light of experience with it. A recording session must be arranged to acquire new utterances. This is especially difficult if more than one voice is used, or if the voice belongs to someone (like the boss) who cannot necessarily be called upon at short notice. It's even worse, of course, if the person has died or left the organization: then everything must be recorded again. Even if the programmer's own voice is used there will still be delays, for you often have to book a computer to use it by yourself if you need to record speech on it. If data compression is employed, a substantial amount of computation will have to be done by the computer before the utterance is in a usable form—this can lengthen the delay before you can try out the new dialogue.

The phonetic input required by segmental speech synthesis-by-rule systems makes life much easier for the programmer. Utterances can be entered quickly from a standard computer terminal. They can be modified easily because they can be edited like ordinary text. The programmer has to learn how to do phonetic transcription, but this is a small inconvenience. The art is easily learned in an interactive situation where the effect of modifications to the transcription can be heard immediately. If allophones must be represented explicitly in the input, as for the Votrax synthesizer, then the programmer's task becomes a lot more complicated because of the combinatorial explosion in trial-and-error modifications.

Plain text input is also quite suitable. You can tolerate a significant rate of error in pronunciation if you can hear the result immediately and adjust the text to suit the idiosyncrasies of the program. There is no need for the system to try to derive prosodic features from the text, because it should be easy for the programmer to put in markers which indicate pitch contours and stress points.

The application of voice response to interactive computer dialogue is quite different from the problem of reading aloud from text. The major concern with reading machines is how to glean information about intonation, rhythm, emphasis, tone of voice, and so on, from an input of ordinary English text. The problems of semantic processing, utilization of pragmatic knowledge, and syntactic analysis do not arise in interactive information retrieval systems. In these, the end user is communicating with a program which has been created by a person who knows what he or she wants it to say. Thus the major difficulty is in *describing* the prosodic features rather than *deriving* them from text. This is much easier to do.

Speech synthesis by rule is a subsidiary process to the main interactive program. In a shared computer system, it is important that the synthesis-by-rule procedure is not interrupted by the computer's other work; otherwise, hesitations will occur at very unnatural places in the speech. In other words, the synthesis process needs to be executed in "real time," without interruption. If the main computer system is shared by other users, the synthesis-by-rule procedure is best executed by a separate computer. For example, a 16-bit microcomputer controlling a hardware formant synthesizer has been used to run the ISP system in real time without too much difficulty. If a dedicated computer is used for the interactive system, it may be able to handle the job of synthesis-by-rule as well as controlling the dialogue. If an interpreted language such as Basic is being used, it may be possible to alter the language interpreter to add a new command, "speak," which simply utters a string representing a message. This makes it very convenient for the programmer to try out new messages, and to alter the interactive dialogue quickly to test new ideas.

With a phonetic representation for utterances, and real-time synthesis in a separate process or computer, it is easy for the programmer to fiddle about with the interactive dialogue to get it feeling right. Each utterance is just a textual string which can be stored as a string constant within the program, just as a VDU prompt would be. It can be edited as part of the program, and "printed" to the speech synthesis device to hear it. There are no more technical problems to developing an interactive dialogue with speech output than there are for a conventional interactive program. Of course, there are more human problems, and we have discussed some of them above.

5.2. USING A KEYPAD

One of the greatest advantages of speech output from computers is the ubiquity of the telephone network. Computer speech allows telephones to be used with no need for special equipment at the terminal. The requirement for input as well as output obviously presents something of a problem because of the restricted nature of the telephone keypad.

Figure 5.1 shows the layout of the keypad. Signaling is achieved by dual-frequency tones. For example, if key 7 is pressed, two tones at frequencies of 852 Hz and 1209 Hz are transmitted down the line. During the process of dialing these are received by the telephone exchange equipment, which assembles the digits that form a number and attempts to route the call appropriately. Once a connection is made, either party is free to press keys if they want, and the signals will be transmitted to the other end. There they can be decoded by simple electronic circuits.

Dial telephones signal with closely spaced dial pulses. One pulse is generated for a "1," two for a "2," and so on. Obviously, ten pulses are generated for a "0," rather than none. Unfortunately, once the connection is made, it is difficult to signal with dial pulses. They cannot be decoded reliably because the telephone network is not designed to transmit such low frequencies right

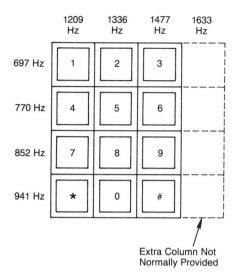

Figure 5.1 Keypad layout for touchtone phones.

through to the other end. However, hand-held tone generators can be purchased for use with dial telephones. Although these are undeniably extra equipment, and one purpose of using speech output is to avoid this, they are very
cheap and portable compared with other computer terminal equipment.

The small number of keys on the telephone pad makes it rather difficult to
use for communicating with computers. Provision is made for sixteen keys, but
only twelve are implemented—the others may be used for some military purposes. Of course, if a separate tone generator is used then you could use these
extra keys, but you would then be incompatible with those using unmodified
touchtone phones. More sophisticated terminals are available which extend the
keypad—such as the Displayphone of Northern Telecommunications. They are
designed as a complete communications terminal and contain their own visual
display as well. This makes them bulky and relatively expensive.

5.2.1. Keying Alphabetic Data   Figure 5.2 shows the near-universal
scheme for overlaying alphabetic letters onto the telephone keypad. Since more
than one symbol occupies each key, you obviously have to use more than one
keystroke per character if the input sequence is to represent a string of letters.
One way of doing this is to depress the appropriate button the number of times
corresponding to the position of the letter on it. For example, to enter the letter "L" you would key the "5" button three times in rapid succession. Keying
rhythm could be used to distinguish the four entries "J J J," "J K," "K J,"
and "L," or alternatively one of the bottom three buttons could be used as a
separator. A different method is to use "*," "0," and "#" as shift keys to
indicate whether the first, second, or third letter on a key is intended. Then

"#5" would represent "L." Alternatively, the shift could follow the key instead of preceding it, so that "5#" represents "L." If numeric as well as alphabetic information may be entered, a mode-shift operation is commonly used to switch between numeric and alphabetic modes.

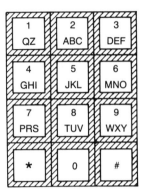

Figure 5.2 Alphabetic layout for touchtone phones.

The relative merits of these three methods, multiple depressions, shift key prefix, and shift key suffix, have been investigated experimentally. The results were rather inconclusive. The first method seems to be slightly inferior in terms of user accuracy. It appears that preceding rather than following shifts gives higher accuracy, although this seems rather counter-intuitive and may have been fortuitous. The most useful result from the experiments was that users improved significantly with practice, and a training period of at least two hours was recommended. Operators were found able to key at rates of at least three to four characters per second, and faster with practice.

If a greater range of characters must be represented, then the coding problem becomes more complex. Figure 5.3 shows a keypad which can be used for entry of the full 64-character standard upper case ASCII alphabet. It was used in a system intended for remote vocabulary updating for phonetically based speech synthesis. There are three modes of operation: numeric, alphabetic, and symbolic. These are entered by "##," "**," and "*0," respectively. Two function modes, signaled by "#0" and "#*" allow some rudimentary editing and control facilities to be incorporated. Line-editing commands include character and line delete, and two kinds of read-back commands—one tries to pronounce the words in a line, and the other spells out the characters. The control commands allow you to repeat the last input line as though you had entered it again, to order the system to read back the last complete output line, and to query time and system status.

5.2.2. Incomplete Keying   It is obviously going to be rather difficult for the operator to key alphanumeric information unambiguously on a twelve-key

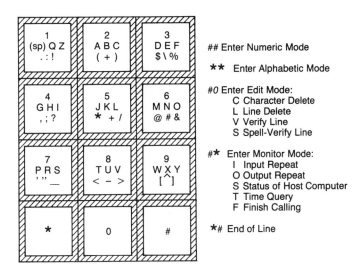

Figure 5.3 Keypad for entering the 64-character uppercase ASCII alphabet.

pad. In many circumstances, single-key entry can be used for alphanumeric data if the ambiguity can be resolved by the computer. If a multiple-character entry is known to refer to an item on a given list, the characters can be keyed directly according to the coding scheme of Figure 5.2. For example, if you key "2455" and I am expecting a common name, it must be "bill." What else could it be? "agjj?" "bhkl?" You can see that "bill" is the only possibility.

Under most circumstances no ambiguity will arise. For example, Table 5.1 shows the keystrokes that would be entered for the first 50 five-letter words in an English dictionary. Only two clashes occur—between "adore" and "afore," and "agate" and "agave." As a more extensive example, in a dictionary of 24,500 words just under 2000 ambiguities, or 8 percent of words, were discovered. Such ambiguities would have to be resolved interactively by the computer system. For example, using the list of Table 5.1, we have

USER:	"22238 # "	(# is the end-of-line character)
COMPUTER:	"Abaft."	
USER:	"23673 # "	(tries an ambiguous entry)
COMPUTER:	"Ambiguous. Do you mean 'Adore'?"	
USER:	"2 # "	(system convention for "no")
COMPUTER:	"Afore."	

Note how the system explains its dilemma and asks the user for a choice. One advantage of systems using speech is that the computer can be sure that the user is present at the other end. Therefore, the system can ask the user for help in cases of ambiguity.

TABLE 5.1   KEYING EQUIVALENTS OF SOME WORDS

aback	22225 #	abide	22433 #	adage	23243 #	adore	23673 #	after	23837 #
abaft	22238 #	abode	22633 #	adapt	23278 #	adorn	23676 #	again	24246 #
abase	22273 #	abort	22678 #	adder	23337 #	adult	23858 #	agape	24273 #
abash	22274 #	about	22688 #	addle	23353 #	adust	23878 #	agate	24283 #
abate	22283 #	above	22683 #	adept	23378 #	aeger	23437 #	agave	24283 #
abbey	22239 #	abuse	22873 #	adieu	23438 #	aegis	23447 #	agent	24368 #
abbot	22268 #	abyss	22977 #	admit	23648 #	aerie	23743 #	agile	24453 #
abeam	22326 #	acorn	22676 #	admix	23649 #	affix	23349 #	aglet	24538 #
abele	22353 #	acrid	22743 #	adobe	23623 #	afoot	23668 #	agony	24669 #
abhor	22467 #	actor	22867 #	adopt	23678 #	afore	23673 #	agree	24733 #

A command language syntax is another powerful way of disambiguating the keystrokes that are entered. Figure 5.4 shows the keypad layout for a telephone voice calculator. This calculator provides the standard arithmetic operators, ten number registers, a range of predefined mathematical functions, and even the ability for you to enter your own functions over the telephone. The number representation is fixed-point, with user control over the precision.

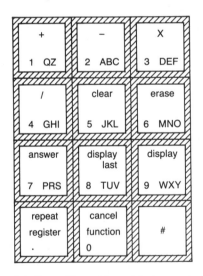

Figure 5.4   Keypad layout for a telephone calculator.

Despite the power of the calculator language, the dialogue is defined so that each keystroke is unique in context and never has to be disambiguated explicitly by the user. Table 5.2 summarizes the command language. A calculation is a sequence of operations followed by an EXIT function call. There are twelve different operations, one for each button on the keypad. Actually, two of them—*cancel* and *function*—share the same key so that "#" can be reserved for use as a separator; but the context ensures that they can never be confused by the system.

TABLE 5.2 SYNTAX FOR A TELEPHONE CALCULATOR

Construct	Definition	Explanation
<calculation>		a sequence of <operation>s followed by a call to the system function *E X I T*
<operation>	<add> OR <subtract> OR <multiply> OR <divide> OR <function> OR <clear> OR <erase> OR <answer> OR <display-last> OR <display> OR <repeat> OR <cancel>	
<add>	+ <value> # OR + # <function>	
<subtract> <multiply> <divide>	similar to <add>	
<value>	<numeric-value> OR *register* <single-digit>	
<numeric-value>		a sequence of keystrokes like 1 . 2 3 4 or 1 2 3 . 4 or 1 2 3 4
<function>	*function* <name> # <value> #	some functions do not need the <value> part
<name>		a sequence of keystrokes like *S I N* or *E X I T* or *M Y F U N C*
<clear>	*clear register* <single-digit> #	clears one of the 10 registers
<erase>	*erase* #	undoes the effect of the last operation
<answer>	*answer register* <single-digit> #	reads the contents of a register
<display-last> <display> <repeat>		these provide "repeat" facilities
<cancel>		aborts the current utterance

Six of the operations give control over the dialogue. There are three different "repeat" commands; a command called *erase* which undoes the effect of the last operation; one which reads out the value of a register; and one which aborts the current utterance. Four more commands provide the basic arithmetic operations of add, subtract, multiply, and divide. The operands of these may be numbers entered directly on the keypad, or register values, or function calls. A further command clears a register.

It is through functions that the extensibility of the language is achieved. A function has a name like SIN, EXIT, MYFUNC which is keyed with an appropriate single-key-per-character sequence. For these examples it would be 746 for SIN, 3948 for EXIT, and 693862 for MYFUNC. One function, DEFINE, allows new ones to be entered. Another, LOOP, repeats sequences of operations. TEST incorporates arithmetic testing. The details of these are not important: what is interesting is the evident power of the calculator.

For example, the keying sequence

5 # 1 1 2 3 # 2 1 . 2 # 9 # 6 # 2 1 . 4 #

would be decoded as

clear + 123 − 1.2 *display erase* − 1.4

One of the difficulties with such a tight syntax is that almost any sequence will be interpreted as a valid calculation—syntax errors are nearly impossible. Thus a small mistake by the user can have a catastrophic effect on the calculation. Here, however, speech output gives an advantage over conventional character-by-character echoing on visual displays. It is quite adequate to echo syntactic units as they are decoded, instead of echoing keys as they are entered. I suggested earlier that each entry should be confirmed by the computer repeating it in the same way that you yourself would be likely to verbalize it. The synthetic voice could respond to the above keying sequence by saying the words shown in the second line. Of course, the *display* command would also state the result, and possibly summarize the calculation so far. Numbers should be verbalized as "one hundred twenty-three" instead of as "one ... two ... three." Notice that this will make it necessary to await the "#" terminator after numbers and function names before they can be echoed.

5.3. TALKING CALCULATOR

Now let's turn from ideas to actual physical devices. In this and the remaining sections, we will look at real examples of talking computers. We start with a simple off-the-shelf calculator that speaks, shown in Figure 5.5. It's much more rudimentary than the one described above. Whenever you press a key, the device confirms the action by saying the key's name. The result of any computation is also spoken aloud. For most people, the addition of speech output to

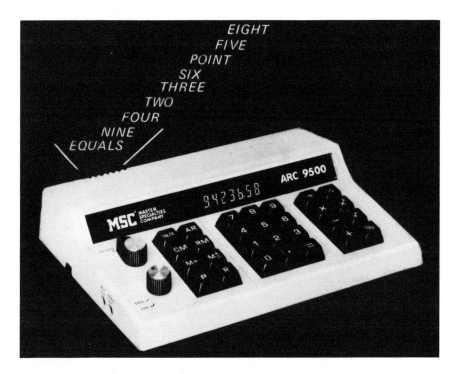

Figure 5.5 Talking calculator.

a calculator is simply a gimmick. (Notice that speech *input* is a different matter altogether. The ability to dictate lists of numbers and commands to a calculator without lifting your eyes from the page would have very great advantages over keypad input.) Used-car salesmen find that speech output sometimes helps to clinch a deal: They key in the basic car price and their bargain-basement deductions, and customers are so bemused by the resulting price's being spoken aloud by a machine that they sign the check without thinking. More seriously, there may be some small advantage to be gained when one is keying a list of figures by touch from having their values read back for confirmation. For blind people, however, such devices are a boon—and there are many other applications, like talking elevators and talking clocks, which benefit from even very restricted voice output. Much more sophisticated is a typewriter with audio feedback, designed by IBM for the blind. Although blind typists can remember where the keys on a typewriter are without difficulty, they rely on sighted proofreaders to help check their work. This device could make them more useful as office typists and secretaries. As well as verbalizing the material and punctuation that has been typed, either by attempting to pronounce the words or by spelling them out as individual letters, it prompts the user through the more complex action sequences that are possible on the typewriter.

TABLE 5.3 VOCABULARY
OF A TALKING CALCULATOR

zero	percent
one	low
two	over
three	root
four	em (m)
five	times
six	point
seven	overflow
eight	minus
nine	plus
times-minus	clear
equals	swap

The vocabulary of the talking calculator comprises the 24 words of Table 5.3. This represents a total of about thirteen seconds of speech. It is stored electronically in read-only memory (ROM); Figure 5.6 shows the circuitry of the speech module inside the calculator. There are three large chips, or integrated circuits. Two of them are ROMs, and the third is a special synthesis chip which decodes the highly compressed stored data into an audio waveform. The speech quality is very poor because of the highly compressed storage, and words are spoken in a grating monotone. However, because of the very small vocabulary, the quality is certainly good enough for reliable identification of the results of calculations.

5.4. COMPUTER-GENERATED WIRING INSTRUCTIONS

One big advantage of speech over visual output is that it leaves the eyes free for other tasks. When wiring telephone equipment during manufacture, the operator needs to use hands as well as eyes to keep the place in the task. For some time, tape-recorded instructions have been used for this in certain manufacturing plants. For example, the instruction

Red 2.5   11A terminal strip   7A tube socket

instructs you to cut 2.5 in. of red wire, attach one end to a specified point on the terminal strip, and attach the other to a pin of the tube socket. The tape recorder is fitted with a pedal switch to allow you to execute a sequence of these instructions at your own pace.

The usual way of recording the instruction tape is to have a person dictate the instructions from a printed list. The tape is then checked against the list by someone else to ensure that the instructions are correct. Since wiring lists are usually stored and maintained by a computer anyway, it makes sense to consider

Figure 5.6 Circuitry of speech module within the talking calculator.

whether speech synthesis techniques could be used to generate the acoustic tape directly by computer.

Table 5.4 shows the vocabulary needed for this application. It is rather larger than that of the talking calculator—about 25 seconds of speech. Nevertheless, it is still well within the capacity of contemporary single-chip read-only memories, if compressed by using present-day data compression methods. At the time that the scheme was investigated (1970 – 1971), however, the technology for low-cost microcircuit implementation was not available. But this is not important for this particular application, for there is no need to perform the synthesis on a miniature low-cost computer system, nor need it be accomplished quickly. The computer can prepare the cassette tape off-line, taking its time. In fact, the technique of joining together previously-recorded words was used, and it was implemented on a minicomputer. The words were stored as parameters for a formant synthesizer. Operating much more slowly than real time, the system calculated the speech waveform and wrote it to disk storage. A subsequent phase read the precomputed messages and recorded them on a computer-controlled cassette tape recorder.

Informal evaluation showed the scheme to be successful. Indeed, the synthetic speech, which sounded quite stereotyped and unnatural, was actually preferred to real speech in the noisy environment of the production line, This is because each instruction was spoken in the same format, with the same programmed pause between the items. A list of 58 instructions of the form shown above was recorded and used to wire several pieces of apparatus without errors.

TABLE 5.4 VOCABULARY NEEDED
FOR COMPUTER-GENERATED WIRING INSTRUCTIONS

A	green	seventeen
black	left	six
bottom	lower	sixteen
break	make	strip
C	nine	ten
capacitor	nineteen	terminal
eight	one	thirteen
eighteen	P	thirty
eleven	point	three
fifteen	R	top
fifty	red	tube socket
five	repeat coil	twelve
forty	resistor	twenty
four	right	two
fourteen	seven	upper

5.5. SPEECH OUTPUT IN THE TELEPHONE EXCHANGE

Speech is now being used in real commercial applications in telephone exchanges. One example is System X, the British Post Office's computer-controlled exchange. This incorporates many features not found in conventional telephone exchanges. For example, if a number is found to be busy, the call can be attempted again by a "repeat last call" command; the number does not have to be redialed. Alternatively, the last number can be stored for future redialing, freeing the phone for other calls. "Short code dialing" allows a customer to associate short codes with commonly dialed numbers. Alarm calls can be booked at specified times, and are made automatically without human intervention. Incoming calls can be barred, as can outgoing ones. A diversion service allows all incoming calls to be routed to another telephone, either immediately, or if a call to the original number remains unanswered for a certain period of time, or if the original number is busy. Three-party calls can be set up automatically, without involving the operator.

When you make use of these facilities you are presented with something of a problem. With conventional telephone exchanges, feedback is provided on what is happening to a call by the use of tones—like the dial tone, the busy tone, and the ringing tone. There is another kind of feedback, no tone at all, which is not supposed to happen, but occurs when the system is confused. For the more sophisticated interaction which you can have with the advanced exchange, a much greater variety of status signals is needed. The obvious solution is to use computer-generated spoken messages to inform callers when these services are invoked, and to guide them through the sequences of actions needed to set up facilities like call redirection. For example, the messages needed by the exchange when a user dials the alarm call service are

> Alarm call service. Dial the time of your alarm call followed by square.†
> You have booked an alarm call for seven thirty hours.
> Alarm call operator. At the third stroke it will be seven thirty.

Actually, a rather small vocabulary is needed. Also, many complete messages can be recorded and stored as a single unit, rather than being formed by joining words or phrases. Therefore, because of the short time which was available for development, System X stores the speech waveform itself, slightly compressed by an encoding operation. Utterances which contain variable parts, like the time of alarm in the messages above, are constructed by inserting separately recorded digits into a fixed "carrier" message. No attempt is made to make the synthetic utterances sound as though they were intoned as a single unit. The resulting speech is very clearly articulated, being a slightly compressed recording of a human voice, but sometimes has a rather strange intonation. For example, the digits in numbers often sound rather jerky and out of context—which indeed they are.

Even more advanced facilities can be expected on telephone exchanges in the future. Take as an example a message storage capability. Although automatic call recording machines have been around for years, a centralized facility could time- and date-stamp a message. It could collect the caller's identity, which would have to be typed on the telephone keypad. Through an interactive dialogue, you could select messages left for you, controlling the order in which you hear them. You could decide to leave some messages to be dealt with later, or reroute them to a colleague. You may even want to leave reminders for yourself, to be dialed automatically at specified times. These would be like alarm calls with with your own information attached. The sender of a message could be informed automatically by the system when it is delivered. Fortunately, none of this needs speech *recognition,* but it does need economical speech *storage,* and also speech *synthesis*—for time and date tags.

5.6. TRAVEL CONSULTANT

There is a world of difference between speech synthesis at work in a real system and the usual laboratory demonstration situation, where people are expected to listen, with interest, to random utterances spoken by a computer. People are prepared to tolerate rather low-quality speech if they feel that the interaction is worthwhile. One step further is the use of speech *input* as well as output, and here the context that the conversation provides can be used to improve recognition accuracy significantly. A system set up in 1979 at Bell Telephone

---

†"Square" is the term used for the " # " key on the touchtone telephone.

Laboratories indicates what we can expect to find operating commercially in the future. It gives timetable information about airline flights, and allows the user to make reservations on them.

TABLE 5.5 A CONVERSATION WITH AN AIRLINE FLIGHT INFORMATION SERVICE

COMPUTER:	This is the Bell Laboratories flight information system. May I help you?
CALLER:	I would like to go to Chicago.
COMPUTER:	Please specify the day of your departure.
CALLER:	I want to leave at four pm.
COMPUTER:	Please specify the day of your departure.
CALLER:	I want to depart on the two five May.
COMPUTER:	Flight number nine two leaves New York at four p.m.; arrives in Chicago at five twenty-five pm.
CALLER:	What plane is on the flight?
COMPUTER:	The aircraft is a Boeing seven twenty-seven.
CALLER:	How much is the fare?
COMPUTER:	The round trip coach fare is one hundred forty-two dollars.
CALLER:	I want a first-class seat.
COMPUTER:	One seat thank you.
CALLER:	What is the fare?
COMPUTER:	The round trip first class fare is one hundred eighty-four dollars.
CALLER:	Please repeat the arrival time.
COMPUTER:	The arrival time is five twenty-five p.m.
CALLER:	I will take the flight.
COMPUTER:	Your reservation on flight number nine two to Chicago on Friday is confirmed. Thank you.

An example dialogue is given in Table 5.5. The user dials the system from an ordinary telephone. The recognition side accepts isolated words spoken with brief pauses between them. It needs to be trained by each user in advance. The voice response unit has a vocabulary of around two hundred words, and synthesizes its answers by slotting words into "templates" constructed by the speech understanding part in response to a query. For example,

> This flight makes . . . stops
> Flight number . . . leaves . . . at . . .,   arrives in . . . at . . .

are templates. When called with specific slot fillers, they could produce the utterances

> This flight makes three stops

> Flight number nine two leaves New York at four p.m. arrives in Chicago at five twenty-five p.m.

The chief research interest of the system is in its speech-understanding capabilities. In fact, the method used for speech output is relatively straightforward. The templates and words are recorded, digitized, compressed slightly, and stored on computer disk files. They total a few hundred thousand bytes of storage. The technique is similar to that used by System X. No independent manipulation of intonation is possible, so although the utterances sound intelligible, the transition between templates and slot fillers is not completely fluent. However, the overall context of the dialogue means that communication is not seriously impaired even if the machine occasionally misunderstands the person or vice versa. The user's attention is drawn away from recognition accuracy and focused on the problem of getting the information wanted. Progress in speech recognition can best be made by studying it in the context of *communication*, rather than in a vacuum or as part of a one-way channel. The same is undoubtedly true of speech synthesis as well.

5.7. TELEPHONE ENQUIRY SERVICE

The computer-generated wiring scheme illustrates how speech can be used to give instructions without diverting visual attention from the task at hand. System X shows how it can be used to help place calls. The flight information system uses speech recognition for input, but its speech output is rather rudimentary. Let's now look at a system which shows how speech output, synthesized by rule, can make the telephone receiver into a remote computer terminal for the purpose of entering and retrieving information. Having first called the computer and waited for it to answer, you use the touchtone keypad shown in Figure 5.7 for input, and the computer generates synthetic voice responses. Table 5.6 shows the process of making contact with the system.

The computer can respond much faster than you can type, especially when you are forced to use the rather unnatural telephone keypad for making your enquiries. Advantage is taken of this to hasten the dialogue by making it a question-and-answer session, with the computer taking the initiative. The machine can afford to be slightly verbose if by so doing it makes the caller's response easier, and therefore more rapid. Moreover, if you are experienced enough with the system to anticipate questions, you can simply type ahead, answering them even before they have been asked. The computer is programmed to check for any input before speaking. As I recommended earlier in this chapter, if it is about to prompt the user and a response has already been obtained in advance, it suppresses the prompt and processes the input immediately. People often take advantage of this by entering their user number, password, and desired service number in a single sequence, taking them straight to the service they require without any dialogue.

An important aim of the system is to allow computer programmers with no special knowledge of speech to write independent services for it. Table 5.7 shows an example of the use of one such application program, the Stores Information Service, which enables you to make enquiries about electronic components kept in stock. These are answered from a database which holds the

Figure 5.7 A touchtone telephone terminal.

TABLE 5.6 MAKING CONTACT WITH THE TELEPHONE ENQUIRY SYSTEM

CALLER:	Dials the service.
COMPUTER:	Answers telephone. "Hello, Telephone Enquiry Service. Please enter your user number."
CALLER:	Enters user number.
COMPUTER:	"Please enter your password."
CALLER:	Enters password.
COMPUTER:	Checks validity of password. If invalid, the user is asked to re-enter his user number. Otherwise, "Which service do you require?"
CALLER:	Enters service number.

appropriate information. Notice that *alphanumeric* data has to be entered on the touchtone keypad, and the method of possibly ambiguous single-key entry described above is used. The letters are printed on a card overlay that fits the keypad, which can be seen in Figure 5.7. You usually need to press just one key for each character. The ambiguity that results is resolved by the computer if possible from a list of permissible entries. For example, the component names SN7406 and ZTX300 are read by the machine as "767406" and "189300," respectively. Confusion rarely occurs because the machine is expecting a valid component code. In the rare cases where there is genuine ambiguity, the computer responds by requesting further information: "The component name is SN7406. Is this correct?" In fact, the Stores Information Service illustrated in Table 5.7 is defective in that it *always* requests confirmation of an entry, even when there is no ambiguity.

TABLE 5.7 THE STORES INFORMATION SERVICE

COMPUTER:	"Stores Information Service. Please enter component name."
CALLER:	Enters "SN7406 # ."
COMPUTER:	"The component name is SN7406. Is this correct?"
CALLER:	Enters "*1 # " (system convention for "yes").
COMPUTER:	"This component is in stores."
CALLER:	Enters "*7 # " (command for "price").
COMPUTER:	"The component price is 35 cents."
CALLER:	Enters "*8 # " (command for "minimum number").
COMPUTER:	"The minimum number of this component kept in stores is 10."
CALLER:	Enters "SN7417 # ."
COMPUTER:	"The component name is SN7417. Is this correct?"
CALLER:	Enters "*1 # ."
COMPUTER:	"This component is not in stores."
CALLER:	Enters "*9 # " (command for "delivery time").
COMPUTER:	"The expected delivery time is 14 days."
CALLER:	Enters "*0 # ."
COMPUTER:	"Which service do you require?"

A distinction is drawn throughout the system between data entries and commands. Commands always begin with a "*." In this example, the programmer decided to define a command for each possible question about a component, so that a new component name can be entered at any time without ambiguity. The price paid for the resulting brevity of dialogue is that you have to memorize the meaning of the commands. This is an inherent disadvantage of a one-dimensional auditory display over the more conventional graphical output from computers. With a television terminal, you often present a "menu" of possible actions at each stage, and users can select what they want to do by indicating an item on the menu. Presenting menus by speech is tedious and long-winded. In practice, however, for a simple task like the Stores Information Service it is quite easy for the caller to search for the appropriate command by trying out all possibilities—there are only a few.

In order to make it easier to memorize commands, some system-wide conventions are established. Each input is terminated by a " # ." There are several standard commands which can be used in any service. These are given in Table 5.8.

A summary of services available on the system is shown in Table 5.9. They range from simple games and demonstrations, through serious database services, to system maintenance facilities. In order to control use of the system, services with high numbers are available only to certain users. Services in the

TABLE 5.8 SYSTEM-WIDE CONVENTIONS FOR THE SERVICE

* #	Erase this input line, regardless of what has been typed before the ''*''.
*0 #	Stop. Used to exit from any service.
*1 #	Yes.
*2 #	No.
*3 #	Repeat question or summarize state of current transaction.
# alone	Short form of repeat. Repeats or summarizes in an abbreviated fashion.

TABLE 5.9 SUMMARY OF SERVICES ON A TELEPHONE ENQUIRY SYSTEM

1	tells the time
2	Biffo (a game of NIM)
3	MOO (a game similar to that marketed under the name ''Mastermind'')
4	error demonstration
5	speak a file in phonetic format
6	listening test
7	music (allows you to enter a tune and play it)
8	gives the date
100	squash ladder
101	stores information service
102	computes means and standard deviations
103	telephone directory
411	user information
412	change password
413	gripe (permits feedback on services from caller)
600	first-year laboratory marks entering service
910	repeat utterance (allows testing of system)
911	speak utterance (allows testing of system)
912	enable/disable user 100 (a no-password guest user number)
913	mount a magnetic tape on the computer
914	set/reset demonstration mode (prohibits access by low-priority users)
915	inhibit games
916	inhibit the MOO game
917	disable password checking when users log in

lowest range (1−99) can be obtained by all, while those in the highest range (900−999) are maintenance services, available only to the system administrators. Access to the lower-numbered "games" services can be barred by the administrators. This was found necessary to prevent overuse of the system! A great advantage of telephone access to a computer system is that some day-to-day maintenance can be done remotely, from the office telephone.

This telephone enquiry service, which was built in 1974, demonstrated that speech synthesis had moved from a specialist phonetic discipline into the province of engineering practicability. The speech was generated "by rule" from a phonetic input by using a precursor to the ISP system described in Chapters 3 and 4. Because of the phonetic input, the data storage requirements are very low. An enormous vocabulary and range of services could be accommodated on a small computer system. Despite the fairly low quality of the speech, the response from callers was most encouraging. Admittedly the user population was a self-selected body of university staff, which you might suppose has high tolerance to new ideas. A system designed for the general public would need more effort spent on developing speech of greater intelligibility. It was noticed that some callers failed to understand parts of the responses, even after repetition. However, communication was largely unhindered in most cases. It is amazing what people can do when they are driven by a high motivation to help the system help them.

Making a computer system available over the telephone results in a sudden huge increase in the user population. Although everyone liked having a new, free, computer terminal in the office, careful resource allocation was essential to prevent the service's being hogged by a persistent few. As with all multiaccess computer systems, it is particularly important that error recovery is effected automatically and gracefully.

A system like this provides opportunities for imaginative administration. Playing games had to be rationed on a daily basis to prevent overuse. Some of the experiments that we wanted to do with the synthetic speech involved rather boring sessions of listening to nonsense words and trying to identify them. To encourage people to do them, we silently increased the games ration for people who did the tests. It was amazing how quickly this was discovered, and soon there was no shortage of subjects! It is clearly very convenient to be able to do listening tests from your office in your own time.

Although the service could be used only from office touchtone telephones, there were lots of calls from dial phones, from people who wanted just to listen to the initial message because of the novelty of synthetic speech. Eventually we made the system give a randomly chosen speech if someone dialed it at night, when it was lightly loaded, and did not enter any touchtone codes during the first fifteen seconds. Of course, it sang carols at Christmas. This led to an amusing incident when someone accidentally left the loudspeaker beside the computer switched on overnight. When an early-morning caller was greeted with the usual Christmas carol, so was an astounded cleaner who happened to be in the computer room at the time!

5.8. READING MACHINE FOR THE BLIND

Perhaps the most advanced commercial attempt to provide speech output from a computer is the Kurzweil reading machine for the blind, first marketed in the late 1970s (Figure 5.8). It reads aloud an ordinary book. Users adjust the reading speed according to the content of the material and their familiarity with it. The maximum rate is around 225 words per minute—perhaps half as fast again as normal human speaking rates.

Figure 5.8 The Kurzweil reading machine.

As well as generating speech from text, the machine has to scan the document being read and identify the characters presented to it. A scanning camera is used, controlled by a program which searches for and tracks the lines of text. The output of the camera is digitized, and the image is enhanced by using signal-processing techniques. Next each individual letter must be isolated, and its geometric features identified and compared with a table of standard letter shapes. It is not at all easy to isolate letters, for many type fonts join together certain combinations of characters like "fi," "ff," and "fl." (These joint characters are called *ligatures*.) The machine must cope with a large number of printed type fonts, as well as typewritten ones. The text-recognition side of the Kurzweil reading machine is one of its most advanced features. In fact, the Kurzweil company was bought out by Xerox, who have started marketing the character-recognition technology for input of documents to computers. They appear to be less interested in the speech synthesis side of the machine.

We saw in the last chapter that it is not easy to generate speech directly from text. The performance of the Kurzweil reading machine is not good. Although it is useful for some blind people—and there are around 250 machines in libraries across the United States—a training period of some ten hours is needed to acclimatize people to the peculiar accent. It is far from intelligible to an untrained listener. For example, it will leave out words and even whole phrases, hesitate in a stuttering manner, blatantly mispronounce many words, fail to detect "e"s which should be silent, and give completely wrong rhythms to words, making them impossible to understand. Its intonation is decidedly unnatural, monotonous, and often downright misleading. When it reads completely new text to people unfamiliar with its quirks, they invariably fail to understand more than an odd word here and there; and it does not improve significantly even when the text is repeated more than once. Naturally, performance improves if the material is familiar or expected in some way. One essential feature is the machine's ability to spell out difficult words on command from the user.

I do not wish to denigrate the Kurzweil machine. It is a remarkable achievement in that it integrates many different advanced technologies. However, there is no doubt that the state of the art in direct speech synthesis from unadorned text is extremely primitive at present. It is vital not to overemphasize the potential usefulness of abysmal speech, which takes a great deal of training on the part of the user before it becomes at all intelligible. To make a rather extreme analogy, Morse code could be used as audio output, requiring a great deal of training, but capable of being understood at quite high rates by an expert. It could be generated very cheaply. But clearly the man in the street would find it quite unacceptable for output from computers, because of the excessive effort required to learn to use it. In many applications, very bad synthetic speech is just as useless. However, the issue is complicated by the fact that for people who use synthesizers regularly, synthetic speech becomes quite easily comprehensible.

5.9. SUMMARY

You have seen the techniques of how to make computers talk, and a small sprinkling of actual commercial devices which use speech output. There are hosts of others, of course, and the application of speech output in computer systems is a very rapidly growing area. Recently announced are some other devices for synthesizing speech from plain text. They can produce better speech than the Kurzweil reading machine. But it is still true to say that they are only really suitable for specialists or handicapped users, not for the man in the street. It is hard to overestimate the effect of the motivation of a handicapped person who has very restricted access to reading material.

At the time of writing, virtually all commercial systems for speech output which are intended for use by untrained people generate their speech by storing human utterances rather than synthesizing it by rule from text or phonetics. The speech waveform is generally compressed by one to two orders of magnitude, for economical storage. We looked at the talking calculator, the Speak 'n Spell toy, the System X telephone exchange—all using stored speech. Most of the messages produced by these devices are recorded as a single unit, and the computer is just being used as a random-access tape recorder. Even when utterances are constructed by filling variable slots in templates, these devices do not often attempt to apply an overall intonation but just accept rather choppy-sounding messages. Because the applications are restricted and do not involve a lot of speech, the user can put up with poor prosodic synthesis.

Commercial talking computers seem to have polarized into ones using storage of natural speech and completely general reading machines. In this book I have tried to show that there is a middle ground—using synthesis from phonetics or even text, but with information about intonation given with the utterance. With our present knowledge, it is really difficult to generate this information from text, because the text needs to be "understood" first. But with a suitable notation such as the one described in Chapters 3 and 4, it is quite reasonable to expect the programmer who builds a talking computer system to specify *how* things should be spoken, as well as what should be said. This is the approach that was taken with the Telephone Enquiry Service.

Of course, such a system is not designed for reading books. But reading general text is not as useful as you might think, because of the difficulty of scanning verbal information. Much of the material we want computers to say is put into the computer for the express purpose of being read back. You can convince yourself of this by thinking about an interactive system that does *not* use speech. All those prompts and messages were typed in by the programmer just for the purpose of that particular system. If speech output were to be used instead, stress marks and intonation pattern might as well be put in along with the phonetic or textual message. Phonetic or textual messages will, of course, be preferred over stored speech because of the ease of entry and modification. Such an approach places a premium on schemes for classifying and representing prosodic features in a way that makes it easy for the programmer to learn how to get the effects that are desired.

The next five or ten years will undoubtedly see considerable improvement in reading machines. But it seems likely that computers will more often be made to talk with human assistance for the interpretive and stylistic choices that are so important in real communication.

5.10. FURTHER READING

Ainsworth, W.A., *Mechanisms of Speech Recognition*. Oxford, England: Pergamon, 1976. Now that you have learned something about making computers talk, you might want to investigate the problems of making computers listen. A nice, easy-going introduction to speech recognition, this book covers the acoustic structure of the speech signal in a way which makes it useful as background reading for speech synthesis as well.

Gilb, T. and G.M. Weinberg, *Humanized Input*. Cambridge, Massachusetts: Winthrop, 1977. There are no books which relate techniques of person-computer dialogue to speech interaction. The best I can do is to guide you to some of the standard works on interactive techniques. This one is subtitled "Techniques for Reliable Keyed Input," and considers most aspects of the problem of data entry by professional key operators.

Lea, W.A., ed., *Trends in Speech Recognition.* Englewood Cliffs, New Jersey: Prentice-Hall Inc., 1980. This up-to-date book covers recent progress in speech recognition. However, it is a collection of papers rather than a general introduction to the subject.

LeBoss, B., "Speech I/O Is Making Itself Heard" *Electronics* (May 22, 1980), pp. 95 – 105. The magazine *Electronics* is an excellent source of up-to-the-minute news, product announcements, tidbits, and rumors in the commercial speech technology world. This particular article discusses the projected size of the voice output market and gives a brief synopsis of the activities of several interested companies.

Martin, J., *Design of Man-Computer Dialogues.* Englewood Cliffs, New Jersey: Prentice-Hall Inc., 1973. Martin concerns himself with all aspects of person-computer dialogue, and the book even contains a short chapter on the use of voice response systems.

Smith, H.T. and T.R.G. Green, eds., *Human Interaction with Computers.* London, England: Academic Press, 1980. A recent collection of contributions on person-computer systems and programming research.

Appendix

Commercial Speech
Output Devices

There is a bewildering variety of speech output devices on the market. This appendix reviews current offerings in order to give an idea of the range available and how it can be organized. However, the pace of change is so fast that any survey is likely to be soon out of date, so I will not attempt to provide anything like enough detail to serve as the basis for selecting devices. The further reading at the end of the chapter lists three recent books which give technical details of a variety of the products mentioned here.

The first section looks at chips which can serve as the basis for "solid-state tape recorders," and at board-level devices which perform the same function but in a more immediately usable package. The next section reviews chips and boards which store waveform-coded speech but can only play it back, not record it. These generally employ more economical coding techniques and therefore can provide more speech per kilobyte of storage. However, you must either accept a standard vocabulary or pay the manufacturer to generate one for you. Then we look at linear predictive and other sophisticated signal processing products. Again, special facilities are needed to encode speech for these, so the following section outlines some services and systems for generating stored vocabularies. Finally, we examine devices and systems which synthesize speech from discrete sound segments. Often equipped with text-to-speech conversion software, these provide the most flexible speech output. However, the speech quality is generally quite poor; much worse than with systems that code and store human utterances.

A.1. SOLID-STATE TAPE RECORDERS

Solid-state tape recorders are an attractive solution for simple, limited applications of artificial speech. Many integrated circuit manufacturers have developed chips which utilize compressed speech waveforms. They perform both encoding and decoding, and are packaged either in a single chip or as a matching pair. They normally use a representation of the waveform called *delta modulation*, either CVSD (continuously variable slope delta modulation) or ADM (adaptive delta modulation). This makes it easy to encode human speech into its delta modulated form, as well as to decode it for output.

However, the price of delta modulation is a higher data rate than methods which use more specialized representations of the speech waveform. Typically, the data rate is 16 Kbit/s, although it can be reduced to as low as 10 Kbit/s and still remain (barely) intelligible. Examples of these chips are

- Consumer Microcircuits FX-309

- Harris HC-55516

- Motorola MC3417/3418

- Toshiba T6831

Most such devices are now implemented in CMOS integrated circuit technology.

Although they are ideal for incorporating into a marketable product, bare chips do not provide the most convenient packaging for many users. In order to experiment with computer speech, it is better to purchase a complete card which plugs into your home computer system. Examples of board-level products are

- Computalker Consultants CompuCorder—for the S-100 bus

- Mimic Electronics Mimic Speech Processor—for the TRS-80

- Voicetek VIO-1000—versions available for a variety of home computers

A.2. PLAYBACK-ONLY DEVICES

More economical encoding is possible with more sophisticated methods of waveform coding than delta modulation. Unfortunately, it then becomes difficult to record your own vocabulary. Standard vocabularies are supplied by the manufacturer. However, the waveform coding techniques are often proprietary and then users cannot, even in principle, generate new words. Since the manufacturer supplies the vocabulary in ROMs, the emphasis is not on the data rate as such but on the price and performance of the complete package. We will return to the problem of custom vocabularies for these systems later.

Available chips which replay speech by regenerating the waveform from a compressed representation include

- National Semiconductor MM54104

- Telesensory Systems CRC

- Triangle Digital Services TDS90

As might be expected, complete cards are often available which package these chips, together with vocabulary ROMs, into a form which is more suitable for use in one-off systems. Other waveform coding systems are not implemented as custom chips but as board-level products. Since recording is not an issue and the vocabulary is stored on the card, the host computer need only prod the device with a word number to make it speak. Therefore the data rate between host computer and device is very low and can easily be accommodated on a standard RS-232 serial line or low-speed parallel interface. Examples of such cards are

- Analog Devices SSP01 — card for MACSYM chassis

- Centigram Corporation LISA — Multibus card with RS-232 interface

- Micromint Micromouth — Apple II card (MM54104 chip)

- Telesensory Systems Series III (CRC chip)

- Triangle Digital Services TDS910 — Eurocard (TDS90 chip).

A.3. LINEAR PREDICTIVE AND SIGNAL PROCESSING PRODUCTS

The use of more sophisticated techniques than simple waveform encoding implies much more complexity and digital processing capability in the output device. Integrated circuit implementations are invariably based on the method of linear predictive coding (LPC), since it involves a regular computational structure which is suitable for fabrication on a chip. This combination of IC and digital signal processing technology was pioneered by Texas with their original Speak 'n Spell chip (TMC0280).

Here is a selection of integrated LPC synthesizers. For vocabulary storage some have on-chip ROM (with off-chip expansion possibilities), others are designed to be driven from a ROM by simple microcontrollers, while yet others are intended for interfacing to computers. Most are implemented in CMOS technology.

- American Microsystems S3610, S3620

- General Instruments SP-0250, SP-0256

- Hitachi HD61885

- ITT Semiconductors UAA1104, UAA1105

- Texas Instrument TMS5100, TMS5200

- Toshiba T6721.

All these products are based on the 10-pole LPC model, except the General Instruments ones, which use a 12-pole model. This makes them capable of higher-quality speech than the others, but at the expense of a greater data rate and consequently more storage requirements for a given vocabulary. The data rate for the pioneering Texas Instruments device is around 1200 bit/s, reduced from a basic rate of 2400 bit/s by clever coding of the parameters used to drive the synthesizer. The data rate depends on how the parameters are coded and also on the speech itself; for all of the above devices it is likely to fall between 1 and 3 Kbit/s.

Instead of producing a special-purpose linear predictive device, some manufacturers have opted for more general programmable digital signal processors. These can be configured to behave as linear predictive synthesizers, or formant synthesizers, or indeed as a variety of other speech filtering or coding devices. However, because of limitations in complexity they are not suited to linear predictive *analysis,* which is needed for vocabulary generation.

- Intel 2920

- Telesensory Systems PDSP

- Texas Instruments TMS 320

Again, complete cards are available which package some of the above integrated circuits, with a stored vocabulary, into immediately usable form. Examples are

- General Instruments VSM2032 (SP-0250 chip)

- Speech Technology Corporation M410, VR/S100 (SP-0250 chip)

- Telesensory Systems Speech 1000, Speech 1100 (PDSP chip)

- Texas Instruments Tinytalker, Superspeaker (TMS5100 chip)

In the case of the Telesensory Systems Speech 1000, the vocabulary is downloadable from a disk, so it can be very large indeed.

A.4. VOCABULARY GENERATION

Acquiring the vocabulary necessary for a particular application may not be an easy task. If the device is a solid-state tape recorder, capable of encoding as well as decoding speech, human utterances can easily be recorded and digitized as required. However, if more sophisticated processing is needed for the encoding process, and especially if the coding technique is proprietary, things are more difficult.

Each chip manufacturer will provide standard vocabularies, often for a variety of different application areas. As an example, Texas Instruments offers the following vocabulary ROMs for its LPC chips:

- VM71001 — 49 industrially oriented words

- VM71002 — 34 words for time-related applications

- VM71003 — same vocabulary with female voice

- VM61002 — 206 industrially oriented words

To show what range of words you might expect to find in a general-purpose vocabulary, Table A.1 gives a list of the 144 words in a standard ROM marketed by National Semiconductor for their MM54104 playback chip (also called "Digitalker").

It is obviously fairly constraining to have to select your vocabulary from a fixed list like this. To allow customers to develop their own vocabularies for specialized applications, Texas Instruments markets the Speech Development System. This is a minicomputer system with a separate microprocessor for speech digitization and data collection. It can generate LPC-encoded data from a recorded human utterance in a format suitable for Texas Instruments LPC synthesis chips. For higher quality speech, the user can edit the LPC data on a visual display, listening to the results and tweaking parameters until satisfied with the sound. Needless to say, this is a very tedious process. The system also includes text-to-speech software which generates LPC data (necessarily of inferior quality) directly from a textual representation. In both cases the data is typically stored in a ROM for use in the application system.

A similar development system called Voiceware is marketed by Centigram Corporation for its LISA waveform synthesis card. In this case it is a Multibus-based microcomputer with a voice digitizer. This system can optionally produce output data in a form suitable for the Texas LPC chips as well.

Many customers will not wish to purchase a computer system for vocabulary development, but would rather subscribe to a service offered by the manufacturer. For example, Telesensory Systems provides a vocabulary generation service to users of its Speech 1000/1100 card. Customers can select from a vocabulary of 2000 words, and can program the appropriate data into 64 Kbit EPROMs, each of which can hold a total of 28 seconds of speech. The charge is modest (around $100 for a 62-word selection). Telesensory Systems is also prepared to develop new words on a custom basis, but at much greater cost (around $125 per second of speech, or about 30 times as much as for standard words). Presumably the standard selection can be expected to grow as customers pay for the development of new vocabulary items.

TABLE A.1 VOCABULARY FOR THE MM54104 "DIGITALKER"

this is Digitalker	e	centi	milli
one	f	check	minus
two	g	comma	minute
three	h	control	near
four	i	danger	number
five	j	degree	of
six	k	dollar	off
seven	l	down	on
eight	m	equal	out
nine	n	error	over
ten	o	feet	parenthesis
eleven	p	flow	percent
twelve	q	fuel	please
thirteen	r	gallon	plus
fourteen	s	go	point
fifteen	t	gram	pound
sixteen	u	great	pulses
seventeen	v	greater	rate
eighteen	w	have	re
nineteen	x	high	ready
twenty	y	higher	right
thirty	z	hour	ss
forty	again	in	second
fifty	ampere	inches	set
sixty	and	is	space
seventy	at	it	speed
eighty	cancel	kilo	star
ninety	case	left	start
hundred	cent	less	stop
thousand	400 Hz tone	lesser	than
million	80 Hz tone	limit	the
zero	20 ms silence	low	time
a	40 ms silence	lower	try
b	80 ms silence	mark	up
c	160 ms silence	meter	volt
d	320 ms silence	mile	weight

A.5. SOUND-SEGMENT SYNTHESIZERS

The problems and cost associated with vocabulary development for speech storage devices encourage the use of synthesizers based on discrete sound segments which the user can experiment with himself. However, the speech quality expected from such devices is much lower than when actual human utterances are coded and replayed.

A number of CMOS chips are now available which use a phonetic-style input. For example,

- General Instruments SP-02560AL2

- Silicon Systems SSI263

- Votrax SC-01.

They are quite similar to the pioneering Votrax synthesizers, of which the SC-01 is a modern integrated implementation. All offer a total of 64 different sound segments. (Notice that this is significantly less than the 80 segments of the high-range Votrax ML-I described in Chapter 2.) They differ somewhat in the provision of control over duration and pitch which is essential for proper synthesis of prosodic features. They also differ in the flexibility of overall timing, amplitude, pitch range, and so on.

For example, the Silicon Systems SSI263, which is the most recent of the three devices above, provides

- 64 sound segments

- . . . each with 4 different durations

- 32 levels of pitch for speech applications, with 8 speeds of inflection movement

- . . . or 4096 levels of pitch, giving 7-octave coverage on an even-tempered scale (for musical applications)

- 16 amplitude levels

- 8 rates of articulation (speed of formant motion towards target values)

- overall frequency shifting for all formants (to switch between male and female formant values, or to achieve "Donald Duck" speech and other special sound effects)

- 16 overall speed settings.

This is clearly a fairly comprehensive set of features for a sound-segment synthesizer.

As with the speech coding devices reviewed earlier, sound-segment synthesizers are also available packaged on cards, often complete with processor and text-to-speech software in ROM. For example,

- DGC Computer Systems DGC Talker — Apple II card (Votrax SC-01 chip)

- Interstate Electronics VTM150 — Multibus card

- Micromint SweetTalker — Apple II card (Votrax SC-01 chip)

- Telesensory Systems PROSE 2000 — Multibus card (PDSP chip).

The DGC Talker includes a software package which adds speech output commands to the BASIC language.

Although built around the PDSP digital signal processing chip rather than a sound-segment synthesizer, Speech Plus' PROSE 2000 is included in the above list because as far as the user is concerned it operates at the same level of functionality as the sound-segment devices. It contains particularly sophisticated text-to-speech software which includes an exception dictionary of 1500 words to cope with pronunciation anomalies.

Data rates to sound-segment and text-to-speech synthesizers are one or two orders of magnitude lower than to the speech storage devices of earlier sections. This permits packaging in a stand-alone box rather than a board which plugs into a computer bus. Communication from the main computer can be through a standard RS-232 serial line or a standard parallel interface (the Centronix printer interface has become a *de facto* standard in the computer hobbies market). Examples of boxed products are

- Votrax Type 'n Talk, Personal Speech (Votrax SC-01)

- Wideband Speakeasy (Votrax SC-01)

- Micro Communications ASCII Vocalizer I

- Street Electronics Echo GP (Texas Instruments TMS5200).

Most include text-to-speech software so that the user has the option of communicating in English text or in sound segments. As with the PROSE 2000 above, the Echo GP is built around a digital signal processor rather than a sound-segment chip, but it is included in the list because to the user it operates at the same level as the other devices.

A.6. FURTHER READING

Cater, J.P., *Electronically Speaking: Computer Speech Generation.* Indianapolis, Indiana: Howard W. Sams, 1983. A light, chatty, fast-moving, and (to me) somewhat superficial overview of most aspects of computer speech output. It includes a useful technical review of 15 or so commercial speech output devices.

Poulton, A.S., *Microcomputer Speech Synthesis and Recognition.* Cheshire, England: Sigma Technical Press, 1983. This little book devotes about equal space to speech recognition and synthesis, which limits its coverage of either. However, it contains an excellent 22-page capsule description of a large number of speech output products from over 20 manufacturers.

Teja, E.R. and G.W. Gonnella, *Voice Technology.* Reston, Virginia: Reston Publishing Company, 1983. Here is a low-level nuts-and-bolts approach to both recognition and synthesis, culminating in an extensive project to construct a voice-operated "ideal telephone." Numerous commercial speech output devices get a mention, but in a casual and unsystematic way which limits the book's utility.

Subject Index